THE
COMMUNITY
COLLEGE

CAREER TRACK

THE
COMMUNITY
COLLEGE

CAREER TRACK

How to Achieve the American Dream
Without a Mountain of Debt

THOMAS J. SNYDER

WILEY

John Wiley & Sons, Inc.

Cover images: Top: © iStockphoto; Bottom © Stephen Hill and Ivy Tech Community College
Cover design: Paul McCarthy

For general information on our other products and services or for technical support, please contact our Customer Care Department within the United States at (800) 762-2974, outside the United States at (317) 572-3993 or fax (317) 572-4002.

Wiley publishes in a variety of print and electronic formats and by print-on-demand. Some material included with standard print versions of this book may not be included in e-books or in print-on-demand. If this book refers to media such as a CD or DVD that is not included in the version you purchased, you may download this material at http://booksupport.wiley.com. For more information about Wiley products, visit www.wiley.com.

Library of Congress Cataloging-in-Publication Data:

Snyder, Thomas (Thomas J.)
    The community college career track : how to achieve the American dream without a mountain of debt / Thomas J. Snyder.
        p.   cm.
    Includes index.
    ISBN 978-1-118-27169-8 (paper); ISBN 978-1-118-28728-6 (ebk);
    ISBN 978-1-118-28360-8 (ebk); ISBN 978-1-118-28500-8 (ebk)
        1. Community colleges—United States.   2. Community college students—Vocational guidance—United States.   3. College student orientation—United States.
I. Title.
    LB2328.S61   2012
    378.1′5430973—dc23

                                                      2012022594

Printed in the United States of America

10   9   8   7   6   5   4   3   2   1

Contents

The Best Higher Education Value in America

1

Why Community College Is the Smart Choice for Almost Every Student

Most people would agree that you need a higher education to have a good life and a rewarding career in twenty-first-century America. But if you think of higher education solely in terms of the traditional model of four residential years on campus, you're setting your sights too narrowly. This viewpoint focuses only on the most expensive, but by no means necessarily the most valuable, form of higher education in America today. It's also one that the majority of Americans simply cannot afford. It ignores community college, a remarkable resource that can provide you with instruction that matches the four-year schools in quality—at a much more affordable cost.

Thanks to plentiful scholarships, need-based grants, and worker retraining funds, countless individuals can attend community college with virtually no out-of-pocket expenses. And most student loans will be manageable ones that you can repay without enormous sacrifice.

If you're a high school junior or senior who wants to start on a bachelor's degree right after high school, you owe it to yourself, and your parents, to consider doing the first two years at community college and then transfer up to a four-year school that will welcome you with open arms. That's what many successful individuals have done, including well-known leaders in their fields such as comedian Billy Crystal (Nassau Community College, Garden City, NY), political strategist Ed Rollins (Solano Community College, Vallejo, CA), journalist Jim Lehrer (Victoria College, Victoria, TX), Stanley Black and Decker chairman Nolan D. Archibald (Dixie State College, St. George, UT), actor Tom Hanks (Chabot College, Hayward, CA), Congressman George Miller (Diablo Valley College, Contra Costa County, California), first woman space shuttle pilot Eileen Collins (Corning Community College, Corning, NY), filmmaker George Lucas (Modesto Junior College, Modesto, CA), scientist and human genome decoder Craig Venter (San Mateo Community College, San Mateo, CA), and architect Frank Gehry (Los Angeles City College, Los Angeles, CA).

Four-year schools, including some of the most selective colleges and universities in the country, readily accept community college transfers; they know these students are well prepared and highly motivated to finish their bachelor's degrees on time. Transfers from community colleges complete their bachelor's programs and graduate at a much higher and faster rate than students who attend four-year schools from day one.

Additionally, if you're a high school student with good grades and a desire to advance in your studies as quickly as possible, you should think about leapfrogging up the higher education ladder by taking dual-credit courses at a community college. You can easily obtain a year or more of college course credit that way, and potentially complete your bachelor's degree in two to three years after high school—instead of the usual four. By demonstrating your ability to do college-level work, you'll likely also raise yourself dramatically in the candidate pools for the bachelor's degree programs that interest you, including the most selective ones in the country.

Are you not planning to earn a bachelor's degree, at least not right away? Then you should look hard at the opportunities you can gain by attending community college. You can prepare yourself for one of America's best jobs in science, technology, engineering, and mathematics (STEM) occupations, like advanced manufacturing and robotics; health care professions and technology occupations, like nursing and radiology; and the best-paid trades, like plumbing and electrical work. Many one-year professional certificates and associate's degrees in these areas will make you far more employable, and bring you much higher immediate and lifetime earnings, than the average bachelor's degree in a liberal arts major. And this is the case whether you're in high school right now, or have been out in the working world for a few years—even decades—as a blue-collar or white-collar worker. If you want to prepare yourself for a great career, or change careers, community college is the place for you.

The traditional model of a four-year residential college experience was never a good fit for most students. Today that model is outright unaffordable for everyone but the most affluent Americans and their families, because of skyrocketing four-year college costs and stagnant incomes. Yet America's unique educational resource, the community colleges, can give you the higher education you need and want. You can achieve and sustain your individual American dream without incurring a mountain of debt.

Transferring, leapfrogging, preparing to enter a highly skill-biased job market for the first time, and changing careers—all of these paths to success run through the community colleges. The following chapters will show you exactly how.

2

Affordable for All

Paying for Community College and Lowering Your Total Higher Education Costs

The Trillion-Dollar Shock

An October 19, 2011, *USA Today* headline announced, "Student Loan Debt Surpasses $1 Trillion." Testifying before a U.S. Senate judiciary subcommittee on March 20, 2012, Illinois Attorney General Lisa Madigan warned, "Student debt poses a large and growing threat to the stability of our economy . . . [and] could very well prevent millions of Americans from fully participating in the economy or ever achieving financial security."[1]

The newspaper headline and the Senate testimony reflected the shocking reality that the average American family, with a median income of around $50,000 to $60,000 for a family of four, can no longer afford a four-year residential college. Americans of all ages have never needed higher education more in order to qualify for good jobs. Yet the traditional four-year residential college experience has never been more costly, and the traditional liberal arts bachelor's degree has never been less valuable.

Fortunately, there is a better, smarter way to get a high-quality education that will serve you well in the job market and in life: attending community college. That holds true for those who want to earn a professional certificate in a year or less, attain a two-year associate's degree or nursing degree, or complete the first two years of their bachelor's degree requirements at community college and then transfer the credits to a four-year school.

Let's start by taking a quick look at how, beginning in the mid-1990s, the traditional four-year residential college experience became unaffordable. The huge increase in college costs over the past several decades has rested on people's assumptions about the value of the traditional college experience—assumptions that no longer hold true in today's world. Unfortunately, people still base their choices on these beliefs, which lead far too many students and families into crippling debt without positioning graduates to achieve good careers and a good quality of life.

■ ■ ■

When I entered college as an 18-year-old in the fall of 1963, college affordability was not a significant issue for middle-income people like my parents. My father was a general supervisor making a modest salary in Delco Remy's automotive parts plant in our hometown of Anderson, Indiana. My mother earned an even more modest salary as a teacher in our local parish elementary school.

We were by no means rich. Yet my parents were able to send my four brothers and me to traditional four-year colleges without spending their life savings or going into debt. My two older brothers went to Xavier University in Cincinnati, Ohio, for four years. My next younger brother and I went to what was then called the General Motors Institute, now Kettering University, which has a cooperative work and study program. My youngest brother went to Purdue.

The schedule at Kettering is a little different now, but the school year was divided up into alternating six-week segments when my brother and I attended. We spent six weeks studying on the school campus in Flint, Michigan, where students mostly lived in a dormitory or in a fraternity house, as my brother and I did. We spent the next six weeks in work assignments at General Motors plants throughout the country. The program typically assigned students to plants in or near their hometowns whenever possible, so that they could live at home with their parents during their work assignments.

That's what happened with my next younger brother and me when we were assigned to work at the Delco Remy factory where our father was a supervisor. Our wages from these working assignments paid for our tuition, room, and board, and our parents helped with our incidental expenses, in addition to providing room and board when we were at home.

The result was that when I graduated with a bachelor's degree in mechanical engineering, neither my parents nor I had any debt connected with my education. I was ready to enter the work world and begin advancing in my career with a totally clean financial slate—and with some "real world" professional experience under my belt.

Cooperative work-and-study bachelor's degree programs like Kettering's remain a great option for many students. But as I'll discuss in Chapter 6, you can achieve much the same work-and-study, learn-and-earn balance by going to community college and combining the low-cost completion of valuable professional certificates, a two-year degree, and/or credits toward a bachelor's degree with increasingly well-paid employment in good jobs.

Even if my younger brother and I had not enrolled in a work-and-study program like Kettering's, the cost of a four-year residential experience at a public college or university in the 1960s would have been manageable for our family. My brothers and I would have needed to earn money in summer jobs and in work-study jobs at school or part-time jobs in the surrounding area, as we all did anyway. But getting a bachelor's degree would not have put us or our parents into serious debt.

Additionally, the return on investment in a traditional four-year college experience was dramatically positive at that time. A bachelor's degree in either the liberal arts or a technical field was the ticket to a variety of excellent jobs. If you were a decent student and didn't go to college in those days, the reason probably wasn't cost. It was simply the fact that there were still plenty of well-paid manufacturing jobs that didn't require a college degree.

Flash forward 20 years to the late 1980s, when my wife, Bobbette, and I began to send our four children—Ingrid, Robb, Matt, and Bekah—to do their bachelor's degrees at public universities in Indiana. At that time I was a mid-level manager at Delco Remy. We had to budget wisely, and the kids had to contribute money from summer and part-time jobs to help pay some of their living and incidental expenses. During a couple of semesters, we took out a federal Parent Loan for Undergraduate Students (PLUS loan) to bridge modest shortfalls in our finances. But we were able to pay those loans off quickly. And we weren't alone. At this time, most middle-income families could afford to send their kids to college for four years.

Flash forward 25 more years to today, as my wife and I consider the prospect of our 10 grandchildren reaching college age. The oldest will be college age in the fall of 2013, the youngest in the fall of 2025. Everything is different now, not only in relation to college costs, but also to employability and lifetime earnings potential. Our grown children and their working spouses are at much the same point in their careers as I was when they went to college. But like most middle-class Americans, they're looking at a yawning gap between their incomes and the total costs of the four-year residential college experience. Those costs have gone up so much that contributions from my wife and me, or others in the extended family, won't be able to make up the difference. In fact, the sticker price for a bachelor's degree at an Indiana public residential four-year college is $72,000. Add books and fees and it will easily hit $100,000—at least $1 million for these 10 grandchildren.

The "Final Four" Syndrome

Like health care costs, traditional four-year college costs have long outpaced inflation. But that trend accelerated sharply in the mid-1990s—right around the time that the majority of jobs began to require higher education. In 1973, 29 percent of all U.S. jobs required postsecondary education. In 1992, 52 percent did. And in 2018, a projected 62 percent of all jobs will require postsecondary education.

At the same time, many students and their families came to believe that a college's cost directly reflected the quality of the education it offered and the long-term value of the degrees it granted. Rankings like those in *U.S. News & World Report* reflected this biased perception and encouraged the public to think that way as well. The mistaken belief that a four-year residential college experience must be the best value is what I call the "Final Four" Syndrome.

Another reflection of this syndrome was that many traditional four-year schools, especially the private ones, entered into a sort of "amenities race." Schools funded expensive new and refurbished student residences, dining services, and recreational facilities as a way of jockeying to be more attractive options than other schools, and to justify revenue-boosting increases in tuition, room and board, and miscellaneous fees. Public four-year colleges and universities also began to hit students and their families with increased costs, as states lowered their funding and sought to make them more self-supporting.

Yet in the midst of what was a seller's market in higher education, middle-class incomes were stagnating when adjusted for inflation. The news media started to notice the financial pain that college costs were inflicting on more and more Americans in the late 1990s. But the economy was booming for the most part, despite periodic recessions and market troubles like the bursting of the technology-stock bubble. Blind faith in buying the most expensive higher education possible paralleled the blind faith that housing values would always rise and never fall. So students kept taking on increased debt, trusting that they'd get good enough jobs to repay them and still be able to afford a nice quality of life.

Except there was a problem: more and more freshly minted graduates weren't getting good jobs like they used to. In fact, the job market was inexorably moving away from graduates of traditional four-year liberal arts programs. Whereas an impressive return on investing in a four-year liberal arts degree was once virtually guaranteed, it became harder and harder for the majority of new graduates to obtain such a return through the 1990s and 2000s.

The full extent of the student debt crisis finally emerged when the housing bubble burst and the economy went into recession. For middle-income families and the country as a whole, it was like getting frostbite. You don't know it's happening until it's so far advanced that you're already going to lose some fingers and toes, or worse.

The Iceberg Effect: Understanding Your Total Higher Education Costs

One of the big mistakes people make when trying to determine college costs is only considering a per-semester tally of tuition, room, and board. Total costs include all direct and indirect expenses: tuition, room and board, books, transportation, recreation and entertainment, and myriad fees. When you consider these total costs, you must also factor in that traditional four-year college costs continue to outpace inflation by a significant margin.

When you do that, you see that the sticker price of a four-year residential experience at a public college or university now amounts to $70,000 or more. They're even higher at private schools, as well as at many for-profit schools. This means that you have to save $70,000 to $200,000 per student to pay for the traditional four-year residential college experience, or else incur a mountain of student loan debt.

Debt loads for bachelor's degrees of $70,000 and more are not uncommon. At this level, student loan debt will likely threaten the ability to retire—or the quality of life in retirement—of middle-income parents who plan to pay off the loans, especially for more than one child. Students who plan to pay off their debts themselves—and who aren't trained in highly compensated fields—will likely have trouble making a good financial start in life, and may have to postpone decisions like marrying, buying a house, and having children.

The financial strain that student debt places on parents and students has a negative ripple effect. If you are struggling to pay off student loans for years, you won't have money to buy or invest in other things. That undermines job and economic growth in general.

Traditional four-year college costs have increased so much that they've not only become unaffordable for middle income Americans; they've become unaffordable for America as a nation.

The Best Higher Education Value in America

The cost-benefit picture at the community colleges is entirely different, from initial and total cost to employability and lifetime earnings power. To appreciate that, consider the following numbers from the Ivy Tech community college system in Indiana. They're typical of the cost structures at community colleges nationwide. It's worth noting that community college costs have not risen anywhere near as sharply as those at traditional four-year schools and for-profit schools, so these numbers should be good starting points for you as you consider your own college costs.

A credit hour—the basic unit for figuring tuition costs—at Ivy Tech is $107.80 in 2012. That translates to tuition and fees of $1,401.40 for a full semester's course load of 13 credit hours. Even after you add $500 for books, you have a basic full semester cost of just over $1,900—not counting expenses for specific course or laboratory materials, incidentals, and room and board, if any.

That means you can complete a professional certificate at Ivy Tech in two semesters of course work or less for $1,500 to $4,000 in tuition and fees, books, and other course materials; a two-year degree for around $7,000 to $8,000; and a three-year registered nursing degree, including its clinical component, for around $10,000. That amounts to less than half the basic costs at Indiana's public four-year colleges and universities. Nationally, community college tuition and fees are only 36 percent of the tuition and fees at public four-year colleges and universities. The savings compared to the cost of more expensive public schools, private schools, and for-profit schools is even greater.

My grown children are looking hard at these numbers and realizing that community colleges can be a smart choice for their children. The cost advantage of community colleges means that you can enter the workforce after college with a modest amount of student debt that you can soon repay—or even no debt at all. But it's not only cost that makes community colleges such a smart choice. It's the quality of the education community colleges offer, a subject we'll explore in Chapter 4. And as we'll also see in that chapter, it's a fact that community college is the best—and often the only—place to study and train for some of America's best jobs. In many cases, therefore, a community college education can make you more employable and enable you to earn significantly more than the average liberal arts major with a bachelor's degree.

Employers regularly tell me that far too many recent college graduates lack the skills that are desirable in today's workplace. And every major manufacturing and high-technology industry is experiencing a skilled-labor shortage. The mismatch between increasing numbers of liberal arts graduates and the job market rests on the widely held but misguided notion that everyone will benefit from an expensive, classic four-year liberal arts education.

This Final Four Syndrome is slowly giving way to the under-standing that it's not where you study that counts the most in terms of employability and lifetime earnings; it's what you study. Chapter 4, which will look at the fields with the best jobs and the routes to excelling in those fields, will cover this in greater detail.

Ivy Tech recently calculated the benefits of attending commu-nity college and found that students who complete professional certificates and associate's degrees at Ivy Tech more than double their earning power. They see average returns of $5.10 in higher future earnings for every $1 they invest in their education, and reap an aggregate 16 percent return on their total education investments of both money and time. This compares very favorably with the current, well under 1 percent return on a standard bank savings account or the 30-year average return on stocks and bonds of approximately 7 percent.

The positive outcomes for Ivy Tech's students also generate impressive gains for Indiana's state and local government, and thus for taxpayers. The rate of return to Indiana state and local government for funding Ivy Tech is 10.6 percent. This includes increases in income and sales taxes and overall economic growth.

In addition, education is statistically correlated with a variety of lifestyle changes that generate public savings. Avoided costs that would otherwise be a drain on public resources and private philanthropy include savings on health, criminal justice, welfare, and unemployment. In 2011, Ivy Tech generated total avoided social-cost savings for Indiana of nearly $22.6 million.

The aggregate benefit-to-cost ratio for Indiana's economy is 33 to 1. The combination of Ivy Tech's impact as an employer and the economic success of its students generates $8.2 billion in annual total benefits to the Indiana economy.

Indiana's experience in this regard is not unique. The community college systems in the rest of the country also make huge contributions to their students' earnings power and their respective states' economic health. Community colleges are without a doubt the best higher education value in America for students and the public alike.

Estimate Your Total Community College Costs

The total cost of studying at a community college will depend on whether you are obtaining a professional certificate or an associate's degree. It will also depend on whether you are a dependent student, with your parents supporting you, or an independent student supporting yourself—and perhaps a family of your own.

Of course, when estimating costs you have to be sure to account for both direct and indirect expenses, which range from tuition and fees to books and transportation. Your individual circumstances may involve expenses for child care or in other areas. You have to write all this information down, or enter it into a personal finance program or app on a computer, and then total it up to determine how much money you will need to attend school.

Before you start calculating your own costs, check the current tuition and fees at the community colleges in your state. You can find these figures on their websites, along with lots of useful information on financial aid.

There are a number of college cost calculators available online. The websites for Ivy Tech and Indiana's public four-year colleges all offer an Indiana College Costs Calculator, and websites for community colleges and four-year schools in other states offer similar tools. But a college cost calculator is only as good as the data you enter into it. Remember that it may not prompt you to consider all the relevant categories of direct and indirect cost you may face.

Think hard about your personal circumstances and favorite activities. You may be able to afford everything you want to do when you are in community college. But you may have to make some tough choices and sacrifice some things here and there.

Don't let that bother you too much, however. The sacrifice will be worth it when you have finished your studies and can confidently apply for the better job, or embark on the enhanced career, that you want to pursue. It will feel even more worthwhile when you start banking bigger paychecks as a result.

Once you've estimated your total community college costs, it's time to look at your resources and potential resources: savings, help from parents, income from current part-time or full-time work, and financial aid.

3

Scholarships and Financial Aid

Merit-based community college scholarships for bright students from families in any income range, need-based grants, subsidized student loans, worker retraining funds—today nearly all students qualify for some kind of financial support for their higher education.

In fact, it is far more common for students to miss out on funds they're eligible for by failing to apply for scholarships and financial aid, than it is for them to hear, "Sorry, you're on your own. You and/or your parents have to pay for everything." For example, the College Board calculated that in the 2007–2008 academic year, 42 percent of the community college students eligible for federally funded Pell Grants did not apply for federal financial aid. (For more on Pell Grants, see the list in the next section.) That's leaving a lot of money on the table.

Apply for scholarships and financial aid even if you think you're not eligible. The strong likelihood is that you are eligible and can get a lot of help in paying for your higher education.

Equally important, once you qualify for and start receiving scholarships and/or other financial aid, make sure that you maintain what is known as satisfactory academic progress or standards of academic progress (SAP). If you don't do this, you will lose your financial aid eligibility. However, you should also know that there is an appeals process for SAP decisions. If you have failed to meet SAP because of significant events outside your control, you can usually retain your financial aid eligibility, so long as you get back into good academic standing. (For more on SAP, see "Maintaining Satisfactory Academic Progress" later in this chapter.)

Find Out How Much Financial Aid You Can Receive

The total amount of financial aid you can qualify for has to do with whether you are a dependent or an independent student. Independent students can receive somewhat more financial aid because their not having financial support from parents makes their cost of attendance higher.

Just moving out of your parents' house doesn't make you an independent student. However, you automatically qualify as one if you are 24 years old or older or are serving (or have served) in the U.S. military. You can also qualify as an independent student at a younger age depending on your individual life circumstances.

Financial aid comes in four forms: need-based grants, merit-based scholarships, loans (they may be need based or open to all), and work-study jobs. Government sources (federal, state, and local), private philanthropic sources, and schools themselves provide a dizzying array of grants, scholarships, loans, and work-study opportunities.

Fortunately, there is one central way to establish your eligibility for practically all need-based financial aid: the Free Application for Federal Student Aid (FAFSA, pronounced "faff-sa"). The FAFSA, a service of the U.S. Department of Education, is a 10-page document with four pages of instructions and notes and six pages to fill out and submit.

As I've already emphasized, you should apply for financial aid, which means doing the FAFSA, even if you think you will not qualify for any aid. Every year students of all ages, both high school students and career changers, miss out on financial aid for which they were eligible, simply because they didn't fill out the no-cost FAFSA.

The FAFSA will determine your eligibility for the following grants, loans, and work-study jobs (dollar values and interest amounts change year by year based on Congressional appropriations):

- Pell Grants: Need-based grants offering up to $5,550 annually in 2011–2012; available to all first-time undergraduates, regardless of age. If your family qualifies for free and reduced lunch at elementary and secondary school, you are most likely eligible for a Pell Grant.
- Federal Supplemental Educational Opportunity Grant (FSEOG, pronounced "eff-see-oh-gee"): Also need based, the FSEOG is for students who have the lowest expected family contribution (EFC; for more on this, see "The FAFSA Process" hereafter) to meeting their college costs. It offered $100 to $4,000 annually in 2011–2012.
- Teacher Education Assistance for College and Higher Education (TEACH): These grants are for those who intend to teach for four years in schools that serve low-income students. They provided up to $4,000 a year in 2011–2012.
- Leveraging Education Assistance Program (LEAP): Federal funds that are allocated to each state for need-based grants and community service work-study jobs.
- Ford Direct loans (commonly referred to as Direct loans and formerly known as Stafford loans): Named for U.S. Congressman William D. Ford from Michigan, these federal student loans were made at 6.8 percent interest and could be made for up $12,500 annually for first-year undergraduate students in 2011–2012. The federal government pays the interest on the subsidized loans until you have graduated, whereas you must pay the interest on the unsubsidized loans from the day you receive the first loan installment.
- Perkins loans: Named for U.S. Congressman Carl D. Perkins from Kentucky, these federal student loans are need based and in 2011–2012 provided up to $5,500 annually at 5 percent interest. They are subsidized, so you do not have to begin

paying interest until you have graduated; however, Perkins loans are generally used only by students attending four-year schools, because most community college students max out their federal student loan eligibility with Ford Direct loans.

- Parent Loan for Undergraduate Student (PLUS): PLUS loans can be in any amount and in 2011–2012 were made at 7.9 percent interest. Because they are unsubsidized, you must pay interest from the date of the first loan installment.
- Federal Work-Study (FWS) jobs: FWS funds underwrite on-campus work-study jobs, and in 2012 provided a national average of $1,465 per student annually.

In addition, states will generally use the FAFSA to determine your eligibility for need-based financial aid that comes from sources besides the federal government. However, most private schools will do a separate need analysis for financial aid that comes from their own institutional sources.

Merit-based scholarships and need-based grants are the most attractive form of financial aid, because you never have to repay them. However, if you fail to keep up SAP, you may lose your eligibility to receive any form of financial aid, whether it is in the form of a scholarship, grant, or loan. And you might have to repay some grants after you graduate if you fail to abide by all the terms of the grant agreement. For example, the TEACH grants become loans if you fail to complete four years of service teaching in a school for low-income students.

Loans can be a crucial part of paying for college, but they should be your last resort, especially unsubsidized loans. Although you can deduct student loan interest of up to $2,500 from your annual income tax, this will likely only make sense if you are in a high-income tax bracket. As a rule, you should borrow as little as possible, and only what you can pay back without its becoming a crippling burden. You also need to maintain SAP to remain eligible for student loans.

The good news is that community colleges are so affordable that you may only need a very small loan, if you need one at all. For example, the maximum 2011–2012 Pell Grant of $5,550 annually was enough to cover tuition, fees, books, and incidental expenses for a full year of study at a community college.

The FAFSA Process

The FAFSA process is more efficient now and easier to use than in the recent past. But there are a couple of big potential glitches that you must be careful to avoid. Here's how the process works.

The Department of Education makes the FAFSA available for the following school year every January (usually, but not always, in the first week of the month). To get a preliminary gauge of your financial aid eligibility, you can use the FAFSA4caster tool on the Department of Education's student financial aid website, www .studentaid.ed.gov. But the FAFSA4caster will not qualify you for any aid. You must complete the FAFSA for every year in which you want to qualify for federal student financial aid.

To complete the FAFSA, you need the following information: your Social Security number, completed tax return for the prior year (unless you did not earn enough money to require submitting a tax return), current bank and investment statements, and current mortgage summary if any. Your parents must also provide the same information if you are a dependent student.

You will also need the Federal School Codes for the schools where you are applying and want your FAFSA results sent. You can have your FAFSA results sent to up to 10 schools. You can find the codes for all accredited schools of higher education that participate in federal student aid programs at www.fafsa.ed.gov.

Once you have all of this information ready, you should be able to complete the FAFSA in well under an hour, allowing time to make sure you've entered everything correctly. But if you have to go searching for information piecemeal, it will take much longer.

You can fill out and submit the FAFSA on the web at www .studentaid.ed.gov or send a paper copy by mail. You can even complete the FAFSA on the phone, if you do not have access to the

Internet or are in danger of missing one of your application deadlines, by calling the Federal Student Aid Information Center (FSAIC) at 1-800-4-FED-AID (1-800-433-3243) Monday to Friday from 8:00 AM to 12:00 AM, Eastern time, and Saturday from 9:00 AM to 6:00 PM, Eastern time.

Of these three options, you should choose do the FAFSA online or over the phone. Mailing in a paper copy of the FAFSA has become a no-no. It will delay the processing of your FAFSA by up to two to three weeks, and the Department of Education is phasing out this option.

If you do not have access to the Internet at home, do the FAFSA on a computer at your high school, the public library, or a community college where you are applying. If you are unsure about how to do the FAFSA, take advantage of the "College Goal Sunday" programs that are available in most states. These programs feature mobile computer labs with financial aid professionals on hand to help you do the FAFSA. Many community colleges have similar days.

One of the benefits of completing the FAFSA on the web or the phone is that you can take advantage of the Internal Revenue Service's Data Retrieval System (DRS). This tool automatically enters completed tax return information into the FAFSA, saving you time, ensuring that the information is accurate, and avoiding a huge hassle in validating the information if it is questioned. Until recently, as I will explain in the next section, you could just bring in your photocopied tax return. But that is no longer acceptable; the tax return information must now come directly from the IRS.

There are a few things to keep in mind about the DRS tool. It becomes available within one to two weeks if you file an electronic tax return, and within six to eight weeks if you file a paper return. This means you should complete your tax return as soon as possible in the new year, assuming you must file a return, and your parents should do the same if you are a dependent student. Your parents must file a joint tax return in order to use the DRS, and if you are married you and your spouse must also file a joint tax return. You cannot use the DRS tool if your or your parents' marital status changes after December 31; if you, a spouse, or a parent files an amended return; or if you, a spouse, or a parent must file a foreign tax return.

To use the DRS, you must first have a FAFSA personal identification number (PIN). If you are a dependent student, your parents must also get a FAFSA PIN. Anyone can do this at www.pin .ed.gov. It takes about three days for a check to make sure you have submitted a valid Social Security number, before you receive a PIN.

You will want a PIN anyway to sign the FAFSA electronically, check your status, have information sent to the schools where you are applying, and manage any financial aid you receive, including student loans. So it makes sense to get a PIN right at the start of the FAFSA process. You will use the PIN throughout your student years and for as long as you are repaying federal student loans.

Once you have completed the FAFSA, it takes two to four weeks for the government to process your application and send you a student aid report (SAR). If you file everything electronically, the turnaround can be as quick as two to three days. The SAR will show your EFC to college costs and your financial need to attend the particular schools that you have listed on the FAFSA. If you don't receive your SAR within four weeks after you file the FAFSA, you should call 1-800-4-FED-AID to check on it.

With your SAR in hand, you can contact the financial aid offices at the schools where you are applying. The school financial aid offices will be your liaison through the rest of the process. Each school that accepts you will send you a financial aid notification award letter, detailing what financial aid you will receive if you register and enroll at the school—and maintain satisfactory academic progress.

Verification

If you see an asterisk next to your EFC, it means that your FAFSA has been selected for verification. The Department of Education selects FAFSA applicants for verification based on an algorithm that gauges the likelihood that they have submitted inaccurate information. The financial aid office at the school you plan to attend must then verify that the information questioned by the Department of Education is correct. About 40 percent of community college students have their FAFSAs selected for verification.

Prior to 2012, financial aid offices could verify tax return information from copies of tax returns supplied by students and/or their parents. Since January 2012, however, a tax return must be verified by the submission of a formal IRS electronic transcript. This is another reason why it is so important to use the IRS's DRS tool when you complete the FAFSA. It guarantees that the Department of Education will not question the tax return information associated with your FAFSA.

Your FAFSA may still be selected for verification based on other information the government believes may be inaccurate. For example, the financial aid office at your community college may be asked to verify information about your household size or the number of dependent children attending college.

Important Deadlines

The federal deadline for completing the FAFSA is June 30 for the following school year. However, state and school deadlines are much earlier. The first page of the FAFSA has a box showing all the various state deadlines. Read this very carefully. Two states, California and Pennsylvania, have special deadlines for applicants to community colleges. Some state deadlines are for dates your information is received, whereas others are for dates postmarked. Several states disburse the federal student aid funds they've been allocated on a first-come, first-served basis until the funds are exhausted.

The FAFSA lists all this information. It even tells you in which states it is advisable to get proof of mailing if you are submitting a paper FAFSA, in which states filing by a certain date will give you priority consideration, and in which states you will need to file additional forms. Schools have their own deadlines, which you can find by contacting them or checking their websites.

The bottom line is that you must know the specific state and school deadlines that affect you. And because of how some states allocate financial aid, you should complete the FAFSA as soon as possible in the year.

The Post-9/11 GI Bill

When you fill out the FAFSA, you will be asked whether you are serving or have served in the U.S. military, or whether a parent is serving or has served in the U.S. military. If the answer is yes, your SAR will include your eligibility for educational benefits under the GI Bill. But you should also make sure to consult the Department of Veterans Affairs website for GI Bill benefits, www. gibill.va.gov, so that you can be sure you know about all the education funding you may be eligible to receive.

FAFSA Checklist

- Know your deadlines.
- Complete required tax returns.
- Assemble all data and back it up.
- Get a FAFSA PIN.
- Complete and file the FAFSA.
- Call 1-800-4-FED-AID if you do not receive your SAR within four weeks of filing the FAFSA.
- After your SAR arrives, contact school financial aid offices.
- Repeat the process every year.

Receiving Financial Aid Funds

You don't have to be accepted at a community college to apply for financial aid. However, you do have to be registered, enrolled, and making satisfactory academic progress to receive financial aid. Here's how that works.

All federal and state financial aid is disbursed on a per-semester basis to the school you are attending. The school deducts any money you owe for tuition and fees (at a residential college this could include room and board), and then refunds the remainder on to you. Like most schools, Ivy Tech does this through a special school-branded debit card that works just like any other debit card and can be used anywhere debit cards are accepted.

Because federal financial aid funds flow to students through the schools, many students mistakenly think that their school can hold up their money and earn interest on it. However, strict federal regulations prohibit schools from doing that. In practice, a school receives federal financial aid and credits it to students' accounts on a rolling basis. There is no opportunity for the school to earn interest on your financial aid dollars before they reach you.

Although financial aid funds will come to you through your school, you can keep tabs on the aid you will receive by using the National Student Loan Data System's website at www.nslds.ed.gov. Despite the name, this system enables you to track federal student aid grants as well as loans. You gain access to the site and your personal financial aid information by using your FAFSA PIN.

Maintaining Satisfactory Academic Progress

To keep receiving financial aid after you enroll in community college, you must meet requirements for satisfactory academic progress (SAP, also known as standards of academic progress). According to the regulations governing federal financial aid, SAP must include three criteria:

1. The student must maintain a cumulative grade point average of C or better.

2. The student must maintain a 67.7 percent completion rate, or "pace" as the government calls it, in a degree or certificate program.
3. The student must complete his or her program within 150 percent of the published program hours.

The second and third criteria amount to the same thing. A 67.7 percent completion rate is the slowest a student can go and still complete a program within 150 percent of the published program hours. Schools can impose their own criteria in addition to these federal criteria.

A student who fails to meet one of the criteria for SAP in a term is placed on warning for the following term. If the student does not return to SAP in the warning term, he or she loses financial aid eligibility.

All SAP decisions are subject to an appeals process, during which students can plead extenuating circumstances. To win an appeal, the extenuating circumstances must be of life-altering significance, such as the death of a spouse or a child, an elder care issue, or if the student suffers a serious illness or injury. Furthermore, the extenuating circumstances must be resolved or the student must be able to compensate for them effectively in the future.

It is up to the school whether to grant appeals. But the school will have to justify its decisions to the federal government during an annual review of its financial aid management.

That said, you should know that the school and its financial aid office are your allies. They want you to be able to complete your education, and they want you to use the appeals process if you have a legitimate reason for doing so.

Transfers and Financial Aid

If you are planning to transfer from community college to a bachelor's program at a four-year school, you need to keep in mind that continuity of financial aid is not automatic. You may also find that the amount of aid you receive does not rise in step with the higher costs you will almost certainly face after you transfer to a four-year school. As part of your transfer planning, you should make it a point to consult the financial aid offices at your community college and the school to which you are transferring. The financial aid advisors in these offices can help you figure out these issues. For more about all aspects of transferring from community college to a four-year school, see Chapter 5, "The Smart Start to a Bachelor's Degree: How to Use Community College as a Stepping-Stone to a Bachelor's Degree."

Looking for Scholarships Online

There are many small and not-so-small scholarships available from varied organizations, foundations, and other sources. It is worth spending time searching online for scholarships with criteria that apply to you. Doing this is tedious, because you have to do multiple searches on the basis of the different characteristics that may describe you or your background. The payoff for this effort can be impressive, however. You may find that you can pay for all of your education this way.

■ ■ ■

Now that we've seen how the financial aid system works, let's look at what you can learn in community college to give you a high level of employability and earning power.

4

It's Not Where You Study, It's What You Study

Why Everyone Should Consider a STEM-Related or Health Care–Related Career, and Why Community College Is the Best Place to Start

The higher education choices you make will have an enormous impact on your life. The most important practical result of these choices is that they will largely define your career and job options. They will almost certainly be the largest single factor in determining whether you can enjoy a good quality of life. With regard to your employability and earnings power, *what* you study has become far more important than *where* you study—or start to study.

I've already introduced the Final Four Syndrome, the mistaken idea that the traditional four-year residential college experience should be everyone's higher education goal. This idea is out of touch with the realities of four-year college costs and median family incomes. The related idea that higher education should emphasize the liberal arts for the majority of students is likewise out of touch with the realities of our fast-evolving economy and job market.

It used to be that the availability of lots of well-paid manufacturing jobs meant that workers who had dropped out of high school or who had no more than a high school diploma could still be part of the middle class. It also used to be the case that a bachelor's degree in any major served as a ticket to a good job. But irreversible trends in the economy and the job market have rendered both of these concepts untrue.

Currently 45 percent of workers who have no more than a high school degree and 33 percent of workers who are high school dropouts are in the middle class—both significant decreases from prior decades. But these numbers are still deceptively high if you take them by themselves. They are skewed upwards by the fact that they include many older blue-collar workers whose accumulated expertise has kept them earning good wages, often thanks to union contracts. When these workers retire, the percentages of middle-class workers who have no more than a high school degree or who are high school dropouts will drop more steeply. Few younger workers in these categories are earning middle-class incomes or can count on continuing to do so.

A bachelor's degree still has significant value. Now more than ever, you must have some postsecondary education to get a good job; generally speaking, the more the better. But what you study has become increasingly important. Workers with a professional certificate or an associate's degree in science, technology, engineering, and mathematics (STEM) can significantly outearn workers with bachelor's degrees in many liberal arts and social science majors. The same goes for credentials in the health care professions and technology, such as nursing and radiology technology. And expertise in trades such as plumbing and electrical work can also command higher wages than many bachelor's degrees (see Figure 4.1).

A bachelor's degree in STEM or nursing will outearn an associate's degree in the same fields. If it leads to a higher degree, a bachelor's degree in just about any field will help you get a better job than someone with less than a bachelor's. But it is vital to recognize that the value of a bachelor's degree in and of itself now depends very much on the field in which you obtain it.

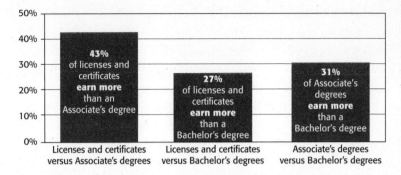

FIGURE 4.1 Depending on the field, a certificate or associate's degree can outearn a bachelor's degree

Victoria Hirsh received a BA degree in liberal arts from Trinity University in San Antonio, Texas, but realized that she really wanted to become a nurse. So in 2010, she enrolled in Alvin College in Texas and earned an associate's degree in applied science–nursing with RN certification in 18 months. Her education cost $5,000, which she paid for by working full time while attending school. She works in the Post-Partum department at Clear Lake Regional Medical Center in Webster, Texas. Nurses in her area earn between $48,000 and $75,000 a year. Her plan is to go back to school and receive a doctorate in nursing practice and fulfill her dream of becoming a midwife.

Whether you are considering community college because you want to obtain a professional certificate or an associate's degree, or because you want to transfer community college credits up to a four-year school and apply them to getting a bachelor's degree, you can't afford to ignore these facts. What you study is crucial to a successful future in the job market. And community college is the perfect place to start working toward that future.

Area of study has become so important because of what economists call "skill-biased technological change." You need a good understanding of this ongoing trend in the economy and the job market in order to make smart higher education choices. But let me first emphasize something I initially mentioned in Chapter 1. Research on the quality of instruction has found no difference, on objective measures, between two-year and four-year schools. You are not sacrificing quality when you save money by attending community college, whether you opt to do so for all of your higher education or only the first part. In this regard, how hard you study is also a lot more important than where you study.[1]

Skill-Biased Technological Change

Skill-biased technological change means that the more technology advances, the more jobs will require technical expertise and higher-level cognitive and problem-solving skills. As this process continues, the more biased the job market becomes in favor of workers who possess such expertise and skills, which they can largely obtain only through postsecondary education. For example, automation of rote assembly-line tasks in manufacturing has made the factory foreman into a process and quality control supervisor, and has turned the assembly line into an arena for process and robotics control technicians. As a result, a growing number of manufacturing jobs require some postsecondary education.

Although the progress of this trend is further along in some industries than in others, it is advancing throughout the economy. Moreover, the occupations and industries where skill-biased technological change is most advanced are the fastest-growing and the best-paying ones. There are no better examples than STEM and health care. By virtue of their being in the center of innovation-driven changes in workplace technology, STEM workers and health care professionals and technicians earn better average wages than anyone except higher-level managers and professionals in the business world. And they experience little or no unemployment; current unemployment rates in these occupational areas are 2 percent or lower, and there is virtually zero unemployment in many STEM and health care occupations.

From employability and earnings power viewpoints, STEM, health care, and other highly skilled job categories form a sweet spot where educational attainment and occupational choice overlap. If you're in that sweet spot, you'll have a much better chance of achieving a great quality of life.

Edward Mass was an unemployed factory worker with more than 20 years of experience as a manufacturing engineer when he decided to take courses at Mott Community College in Flint, Michigan, to get an associate in applied science degree in computer-aided drafting and design (CADD). CADD basically involves the use of computer-aided design software to make plans and drawings, used by workers in construction and manufacturing companies. The U.S. Bureau of Labor Statistics reports that CADD is one of the hottest fields in the engineering arena—even in a sluggish economy. Edward now works for General Electric in Louisville, Kentucky, as a senior advanced tooling engineer. "Attaining this degree has changed my life forever," Mass says. "The interviewers at GE were very impressed that at the age of 65, I went back to school, and I feel this fact influenced them in their decision to hire me."

Jobs and Education

The U.S. economy lost 7.8 million net jobs in the recession that began in December 2007. Although the economy has started growing modestly since then, it is not projected to restore all those lost jobs and begin adding net new jobs until 2015.

But that doesn't mean there won't be any jobs opening up. In both good times and bad, most job openings are replacement positions that become available because of retirement and other departures from the workforce. From 2008 to 2018, according to labor economist Anthony Carnevale and his research colleagues at Georgetown University's Center on Education and the Workforce, there will be 46.9 million job openings, with 32.5 million being replacement jobs and 14.4 million being new jobs (see Figure 4.2).

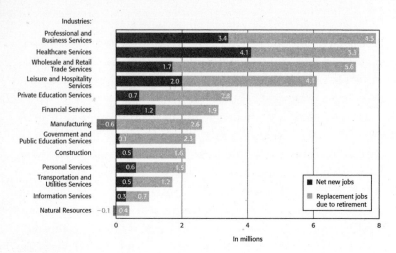

FIGURE 4.2   New jobs and replacement jobs through 2018 by industry

The need to replace retiring workers means that there will be sizeable numbers of jobs even in industries where the total number of workers is declining. For example, there will be 2 million job openings in manufacturing, despite the fact that total manufacturing employment will drop by 600,000 jobs.

As I've already indicated, the crucial factor in obtaining the best of these jobs will be postsecondary education in a desirable field of study. In manufacturing that will mean certificates in advanced manufacturing and robotics control. In manufacturing and many other industries it will also mean STEM-related associate's, bachelor's, and higher degrees. In health care it will mean nursing degrees and medical technology certificates, as well as medical degrees.

Overall, Carnevale and colleagues estimate that 63 percent of all American jobs will require postsecondary education by 2018. They also predict that, counting both associate's degrees and bachelor's degrees, the job market will have a shortfall of 3 million college graduates by 2018.

Of course, this picture will vary state by state, but no matter where you hope to live and work in the United States, more

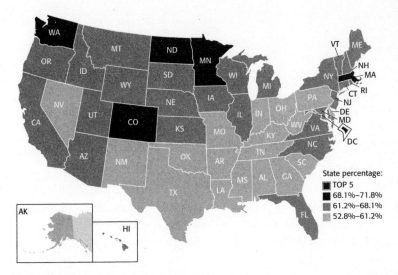

FIGURE 4.3 More than half of all jobs will require postsecondary education in 2018

than half of all jobs will require postsecondary education (see Figure 4.3). More than 61 percent of jobs in 32 states will require postsecondary education. This number will jump to 70 percent in five states: Colorado, Massachusetts, Minnesota, North Dakota, and Washington.

Now let's look more closely at the advantages that workers in STEM and in health care professions and technologies have, and will continue to have, compared to practically all other workers.

The STEM Advantage

You may have heard some conflicting information about STEM occupations. Some people argue that the United States has a shortage of STEM workers, whereas others argue that it doesn't. My experience as a business executive and as president of Ivy Tech is that there is a persistent, innovation-driven shortage of STEM workers in the neighborhood of 5 percent or more. This is enough to ensure continuing opportunity for increasing numbers of STEM workers.

As Anthony Carnevale has noted, the strongest evidence that STEM workers are in short supply is that their wages are rising faster than those of all other workers—except the top managers and professionals in the business world and the top health care professionals. I believe he has also pinpointed the reason for the conflicting arguments, which is that STEM workers are sought after not only for core STEM occupations, such as research and development, but for many non-STEM industries and occupations. If you only count core STEM occupations, you can think that there is no shortage of STEM workers. But if you count all the jobs where STEM skills are valuable, you can see why the economy needs more STEM workers—and will continue to do so.

In an economy in which more and more people need to be knowledge workers, the knowledge and cognitive skills of STEM workers are highly valuable. Non-STEM industries and occupations "poach STEM talent," in Anthony Carnevale's words, because "doctors, managers, and other professionals utilize a similar set of baseline competencies in science and math." This "diverts [STEM talent] from STEM careers before college, in college, and at several points in the workplace. We are not producing enough students capable of filling all these occupations simultaneously."

From 1980 to 2008, total U.S. employment rose 44 percent. Over the same period, STEM employment in STEM occupations grew 175 percent. But showing that non-STEM occupations have indeed been poaching from STEM occupations, the employment of highly skilled STEM talent grew 73 percent in managerial and professional occupations and 79 percent in health care professional occupations.

Those were boom decades for the U.S. economy, of course. So it is equally remarkable that STEM employment growth was the first to recover from the 2007–2009 recession. Only health care, which continued to add jobs throughout the recession, has had a higher rate of employment growth.

The total of all U.S. jobs will grow 10 percent over the decade from 2008 to 2018, according to calculations by Anthony Carnevale and colleagues. By contrast, the number of STEM jobs will grow 17 percent.

These jobs are very well paid. At the bachelor's level and below, STEM workers earn an average of $14,000 a year more than non-STEM workers with the same credentials. Whether they are in STEM or non-STEM occupations, STEM majors with a bachelor's degree or higher have a lifetime earnings advantage of at least $300,000 over non-STEM majors.

STEM workers with less than a bachelor's degree also share the wealth. Recall that STEM workers with some college to an associate's degree can outearn workers with bachelor's degrees in many social science and liberal arts majors. For example, Carnevale and colleagues have shown that "a worker with some college or a postsecondary vocational certificate who works in an engineering and engineering technician occupation earns $29,000 per year more than a worker with a bachelor's degree who works as a high school teacher. . . . STEM workers earn family-sustaining earnings at all levels of educational attainment." You can see this clearly in Table 4.1.

One additional advantage of STEM careers is that, by many measures, they represent the most egalitarian part of the job market. Across all job categories, there are wage gaps for African Americans and Latinos as compared to white workers in the same jobs. However, those gaps are smaller in STEM occupations than in non-STEM occupations, which makes the playing field more level than in the rest of the job market.

Unfortunately, there is currently a bigger gender wage gap for STEM workers than for non-STEM workers. But I believe this will change as more women enter STEM occupations. Community colleges are already contributing to that change.

Financially and academically, Kellogg Community College (KCC) in Battle Creek, Michigan, made sense to Sarah Hubert. She received scholarship aid so that her two-and-a-half years at KCC

TABLE 4.1 STEM earnings by occupation and education level

	High School Graduates	Some College/No Degree	Associate's	Bachelor's	Graduate
Computer Scientists and Systems Analysts	$48,800	$52,700	$57,900	$68,900	$73,200
Computer Programmers	$56,900	$55,800	$56,300	$65,800	$70,000
Computer Software Engineers	$62,800	$68,400	$65,100	$76,700	$84,500
Computer Support Specialists	$41,800	$43,400	$47,300	$52,000	$61,500
Database Administrators	$51,600	$57,800	$50,700	$67,400	$74,600
Network and Computer Systems Administrators	$53,400	$49,400	$51,300	$57,500	$70,700
Network Systems and Data Communications Analysts		$53,800	$53,900	$61,900	$64,000
Actuaries		$128,500	$120,000	$109,900	$130,500
Mathematicians					$73,800
Operations Research Analysts	$53,600	$49,400	$56,700	$60,600	$69,700
Statisticians				$64,600	$72,900
Miscellaneous Mathematical Science Occupations, Including Mathematicians and Statisticians					
Architects, Except Naval	$50,600	$49,600	$74,100	$71,700	$79,900
Surveyors, Cartographers, and Photogrammetrists		$42,600	$50,900	$47,800	$44,800
Aerospace Engineers	$73,400	$89,900	$74,500		$89,200

	High School Graduates	Some College/ No Degree	Associate's	Bachelor's	Graduate
Agricultural Engineers				$74,400	$76,700
Biomedical and Agricultural Engineers					
Chemical Engineers			$76,700	$84,900	$104,100
Civil Engineers		$64,100	$55,200	$71,100	$83,600
Computer Hardware Engineers		$59,300	$59,000	$80,800	$96,900
Electrical and Electronics Engineers	$59,900	$69,700	$61,900	$79,000	$96,900
Environmental Engineers				$76,500	$93,400
Industrial Engineers, Including Health and Safety	$55,600	$51,200	$61,800	$72,000	$84,700
Marine Engineers and Naval Architects				$80,900	$89,400
Materials Engineers				$80,400	$73,400
Mechanical Engineers		$64,700	$61,700	$73,700	$80,400
Mining and Geological Engineers, Including Mining Safety Engineers				$83,300	
Nuclear Engineers				$99,400	$95,500
Petroleum, Mining and Geological Engineers, Including Mining Safety Engineers				$92,200	$78,500
Miscellaneous Engineers, Including Nuclear Engineers	$56,800	$61,500	$64,700	$77,500	$86,600
Drafters		$43,400	$42,300	$39,600	$48,100
Engineering Technicians, Except Drafters	$43,700	$45,500	$49,000	$44,400	$69,500

(continued)

TABLE 4.1 STEM earnings by occupation and education level (*continued*)

	High School Graduates	Some College/No Degree	Associate's	Bachelor's	Graduate
Surveying and Mapping Technicians	$43,700	$35,900	$43,500	$38,200	
Agricultural and Food Scientists	$30,900		$37,700	$46,500	$48,100
Biological Scientists				$44,000	$55,600
Conservation Scientists and Foresters				$47,200	$60,000
Medical Scientists				$57,200	$69,200
Astronomers and Physicists				$61,000	$88,400
Atmospheric and Space Scientists				$62,400	$69,900
Chemists and Materials Scientists		$41,900	$52,700	$59,800	$71,500
Environmental Scientists and Geoscientists	$39,700	$43,700		$60,100	$73,700
Physical Scientists, All Other				$47,600	$73,700
Agricultural and Food Science Technicians		$39,500	$39,500	$43,800	
Biological Technicians	$33,100			$35,400	
Chemical Technicians	$38,400	$46,600	$41,400	$43,100	
Geological and Petroleum Technicians				$35,800	
Nuclear Technicians					
Miscellaneous Life, Physical, and Social Science Technicians, Including Social Science Research Assistants and Nuclear Technicians	$32,200	$31,200	$37,800	$32,400	$42,200

Source: Georgetown University Center on Education and the Workforce.

were covered. After earning two associate's degrees, one in general studies and the other in science, Sarah enrolled at Western Michigan University, majoring in physics. She hopes to receive her undergraduate degree in 2013 and then go on to earn a PhD in physics. Her goal is to either teach in a university or do research.

As a woman studying physics, Sarah is often the only female in her classes at Western Michigan University. She credits her community college education for the confidence that enables her to speak up in class and share her thoughts, ideas, and questions. "KCC has a diverse student body and teaches students to have an open mind," she observed.

The Health Care Advantage

It's no secret that physicians can earn high incomes. But non-MD health care professionals and technicians also enjoy advantages similar to those of STEM workers.

In terms of total jobs, non-MD health care employment growth will be second only to professional and business services from 2010 to 2020. But at 30 percent, the rate of growth will be faster than in all other sectors according to Georgetown University labor economist Anthony Carnevale and colleagues. Health care is the only sector that added net new jobs even during the 2007–2009 recession. At the bachelor's degree level and below, health care professional and technician wages do not match those of STEM wages, but they are excellent nonetheless, as Figure 4.4 shows.

Health care support positions—jobs like nurse's aides, orderlies, attendants, and home health aides—do not pay quite so well, showing average annual earnings under $30,000 in 2008. But we see strong signs at Ivy Tech that this is changing. People entering these jobs are increasingly using them as a gateway to more specialized jobs in health care, and health care support itself seems poised to specialize in the years ahead.

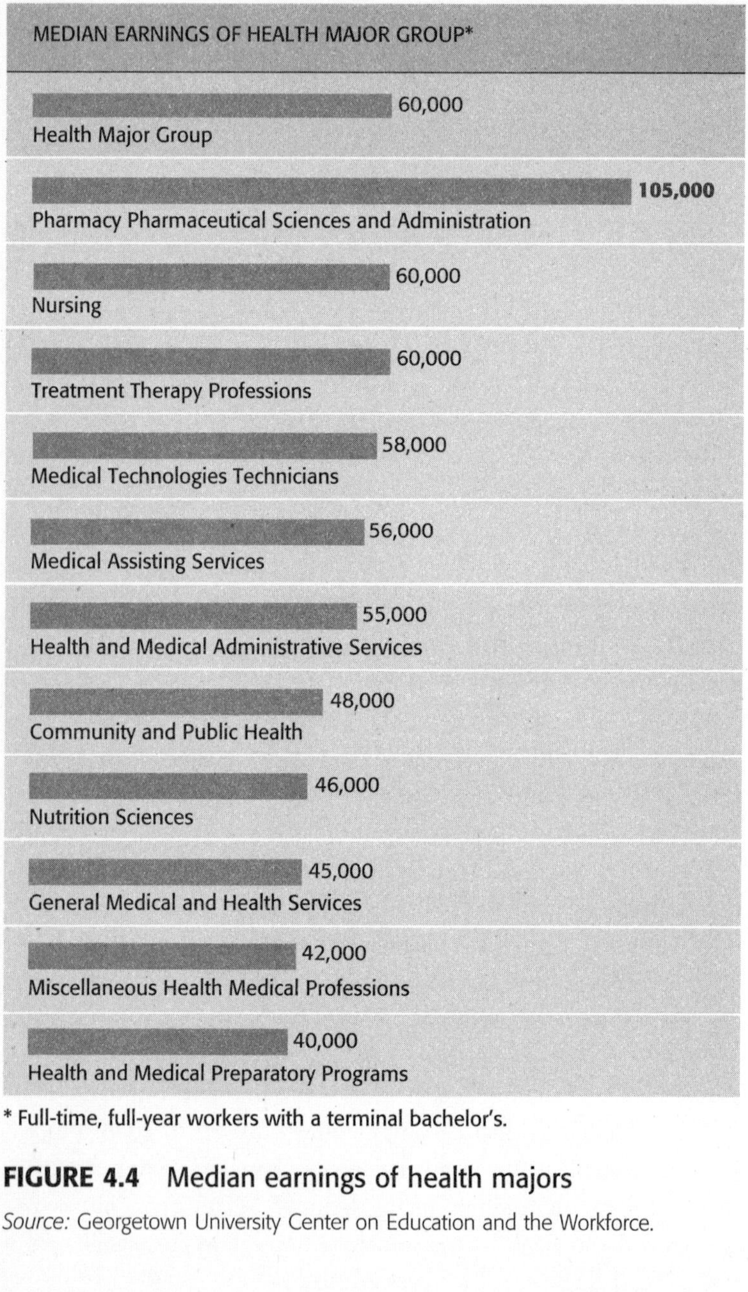

MEDIAN EARNINGS OF HEALTH MAJOR GROUP*

60,000
Health Major Group

105,000
Pharmacy Pharmaceutical Sciences and Administration

60,000
Nursing

60,000
Treatment Therapy Professions

58,000
Medical Technologies Technicians

56,000
Medical Assisting Services

55,000
Health and Medical Administrative Services

48,000
Community and Public Health

46,000
Nutrition Sciences

45,000
General Medical and Health Services

42,000
Miscellaneous Health Medical Professions

40,000
Health and Medical Preparatory Programs

* Full-time, full-year workers with a terminal bachelor's.

FIGURE 4.4   Median earnings of health majors

Source: Georgetown University Center on Education and the Workforce.

You CAN Do the Math

One of the problems with filling both STEM jobs and the science- and math-based jobs in health care and other industries is that many STEM-capable students choose non-STEM majors. Some of this is undoubtedly based on unnecessary math anxiety. Many students who have STEM-capable math scores on the SAT or the ACT mistakenly assume that they haven't scored high enough to be able to get through STEM-major course work. And some students who have scored better on the critical reading and writing parts of the SAT think this indicates that they should not choose a STEM major, even if they might otherwise be interested in pursuing a STEM-related career. There are a host of other assumptions that students bring to this decision, based on their backgrounds and experiences, that keep them out of STEM.

According to data from Anthony Carnevale and colleagues at Georgetown University's Center on Education and the Workforce, fully three-fourths of those who score at the top quartile on the ACT and SAT math tests do not go into STEM majors. And if you set the parameters a little wider, and compare the average math SAT scores of those intending to be STEM majors and those intending to be non-STEM majors, you find something really remarkable. Those opting for STEM and those opting for the liberal arts have pretty much the same scores. It's really worth looking at that comparison in detail (see Table 4.2).

The upshot of this is that many people who could thrive in STEM-related or health care–related occupations are missing out on that possibility. Given the extraordinary earning power of both STEM and health care occupations, you owe it to yourself to ask whether you shouldn't make one of them the main focus of your higher education.

Consider the stories of Dolores Petroulos, Tenaha Williams, and Heather Naugler, who did just that in community college.

TABLE 4.2 Average mathematics SAT score by intended major

Fields	Intended College Major	Mathematics SAT Score (2008–2009)
STEM Fields	Engineering technologies/ techniques	511
	Biological sciences	557
	Computer or information sciences	533
	Engineering	582
	Mathematics	613
Non-STEM Fields	Foreign/classical languages	545
	Legal professions and studies	530
	Language and literature	532
	Multi/interdisciplinary studies	594

Source: Digest of Education Statistics 2009.

Dolores Petroulos retired as a police officer in Orlando, Florida, after 28 years of service, and decided at the age of 55 that she was up for a new challenge. She graduated from community college with two associate's degrees: one in General Studies and the other in Computer Science and Programming Analysis. Despite having dyslexia, she was an honors student. With a $9,000 scholarship from NASA's Undergraduate Research Program, she became an intern at the Johnson Space Center in Houston. While there, she developed, tested, and used simulation software for the next autonomous moon lander. She is now pursuing a BA degree in Computer Science at Rollins College in Florida, and plans on getting a master's and doctorate degrees in either robotics or artificial intelligence.

At Mott Community College in Flint, Michigan, one of the most popular degrees is the Occupational Therapy Assistant (OTA) program. Estimated median salaries for occupational therapy assistants start at $43,910 in Michigan with only an associate's degree. Tenaha Williams worked in the kitchen at the McLaren Regional Medical Center and decided to pursue a degree in OTA. Her ultimate goal is to manage a clinic that provides both physical and occupational therapy services. "It takes a lot of hard work, dedication and motivation to keep going. I wanted to be more marketable and help people and this degree will enable me to do both," she says.

Many times an employer will pay for a worker to go to a community college for additional training. That was the case for Heather Naugler who started working at the Delphi Plant in Flint, Michigan, in 2006, where she checked malfunctioning circuit boards and components. She was promoted to electronics technician, and Delphi offered to pay for her continuing education at Mott Community College. She has now completed an electronics degree and is considering going back to school for a BS in engineering.

■ ■ ■

As you can see, preparing for a STEM-related or health care–related career can vastly expand your opportunities in life. Although what you study is much more important than where you study—and all the relevant data prove that this is so—it's also true that community colleges are often the best places to prepare for certain STEM- and health care–related occupations.

In Chapter 2, I mentioned my "learn and earn" experience as a student at Kettering University and said that you can find similar opportunities at community colleges. That intersects with STEM in the National Science Foundation–sponsored advanced technological education centers (ATECs). There are 36 ATECs around the country in six subject areas: advanced manufacturing technologies; agricultural, energy, and environmental technologies; biotechnology and chemical processes; electronics, micro- and nanotechnologies; engineering technologies; and information, geospatial, and security technologies.

Each ATEC brings together community colleges and private industry to offer the latest in technological education and workforce training. Through ATEC programs you can pursue an associate's degree or professional certificate while also getting paid apprentice experience. For a list of the 36 ATECs, see the "Additional Resources" Appendix.

Great Community College Options—and You Can Choose More Than One

5

The Smart Start to a Bachelor's Degree

How to Use Community College as a Stepping-Stone to a Bachelor's Degree

It's a startling fact that all higher-education consumers should know. Tuition and fees at public four-year colleges and universities currently average three times the cost of community college, and more than six times the cost if you include room and board. Given these statistics, it's no wonder that students are transferring from community college to bachelor's degree programs at four-year schools with increasing frequency. Doing so enables them (and their families) to enjoy extraordinary financial savings.

But the rationale for transferring from community college to a four-year school is not just financial. The equality of instruction at two-year and four-year schools is the other component that makes community college the smart way to start earning a bachelor's degree. Taken together these two elements—low cost and high quality—are why I believe that community college may be my own grandchildren's—and countless other young people's—best first higher education choice as they reach college age.

Individuals who are approaching college age should remember another important factor. You can transfer from community college to some of the best four-year schools in the country. *U.S. News & World Report*'s list of the 100 four-year schools taking the most transfer students, including community college students, features several schools in the magazine's ranking of the top 50 national universities, including the University of California—Berkeley, UCLA, the University of Texas—Austin, and the University of Washington. The list also includes such top 100 national universities as the University of Maryland—College Park, Ohio State University, the University of Florida, and the University of Minnesota—Twin Cities (http://colleges.usnews.rankingsandreviews.com/best-colleges). The Ivy League schools, those known as the Little Ivies (Amherst, Wesleyan, and Williams), and other highly selective schools such as Bates, Bryn Mawr, Colby, Haverford, Stanford, Swarthmore, Tufts, and the University of Chicago also all regularly admit transfer students from community colleges.

The Jack Kent Cooke Foundation has devoted a major part of its attention and funding to increasing the number of transfers from community colleges to the nation's top four-year schools. It gives generous scholarships of up to $30,000 a year to high-achieving community college students to help them succeed as transfer students. To identify scholarship candidates, the foundation works in partnership with Phi Theta Kappa, the community college counterpart to Phi Beta Kappa, as well as other organizations. The foundation also makes grants of up to $1 million to four-year schools that accept community college students into their bachelor's degree programs. The schools receiving these grants include the University of California—Berkeley, the University of Michigan, the University of North Carolina, Amherst, Bryn Mawr, and Cornell.

Steve Crist of Valencia College in Orlando, Florida, worked 20 hours a week at Disney World while pursuing his goal of eventually receiving a law degree. Valencia gave him $2,000 in scholarship money and he took out $19,000 in student loans. He wanted to demonstrate to the bank that he was a good credit risk so that he could get an associate's degree in liberal arts and then transfer to a four-year institution.

He is now attending Emory University in Atlanta on a full scholarship from the Jack Kent Cooke Foundation that his

Valencia professors urged him to apply for. He hopes to graduate with honors and attend law school.

Recently the national media have begun to pay attention to community colleges as a pathway to four-year schools. An April 15, 2012, *New York Times* article noted that two students who were about to graduate with associate's degrees at the Community College of Philadelphia were transferring to the University of Pennsylvania, one student was transferring to the University of North Carolina, and nine students were transferring to Bryn Mawr. Placing this in wider context, the article cited transfers from community colleges in New Jersey and New York to Mount Holyoke College, Stanford University, and Georgetown University.[1]

The students who are transferring are not just from families and backgrounds that are relatively disadvantaged in educational and financial terms. They also come from backgrounds where they would previously have been expected to go straight from high school to a four-year school. Showing that starting bachelor's degree work by earning an associate's degree is becoming an accepted strategy for more and more students, the *Times* reporter wrote, "Indeed, one of my own sons graduated from our local community college and . . . entered New York University as a junior."[2]

Consider Javier Figueras, a young man from Miami who entered Miami Dade College's honors program as an 18-year-old high school graduate in fall 2010. By spring 2012, Javier had earned his associate's degree in business administration and gained acceptance to the University of North Carolina–Chapel Hill as a junior beginning in fall 2012.

I've noted that community colleges are the best higher education value in America. In that context, community college honors programs are the best of the best—and an especially good start to a bachelor's degree. At a fraction of the cost of elite four-year schools, they provide students with intellectually rich and rewarding experiences, often in specially designed courses that amount to having an entire program's worth of small seminars with master teachers.

The country's leading community college honors programs—among others are those at Miami Dade College, Texas's Houston Community College and Austin Community College, Northwestern Michigan College, and in the Phoenix, Arizona, area the Maricopa Community Colleges, including their online institution, Rio Salado College—represent a challenging course of study by any measure. Succeed in one of them, however, and you will prepare yourself to excel in the most demanding bachelor's degree programs. Many community college honors programs have special transfer relationships with highly selective four-year schools.

At Ivy Tech we recently inaugurated our own honors program with a cohort of 24 students. The performance of both student and faculty participants has exceeded our expectations, and I believe the program will soon join the list of the best such programs nationwide.

If the community colleges in your area do not yet have honors programs, they will almost certainly have a chapter of Phi Theta Kappa, the community college counterpart of the Phi Beta Kappa honor society for intellectual achievement. Four-year schools recognize the substantial achievement that Phi Theta Kappa membership represents, and they are putting an increasing emphasis on attracting Phi Theta Kappa members as transfer students. More than 735 four-year colleges and universities offer Phi Theta Kappa members-only transfer scholarships. You can learn more about Phi Theta Kappa at your community college or at the organization's website, www.ptk.org.

■ ■ ■

About one-third of all two-year and four-year college students transfer at some point during their undergraduate studies. This number includes lots of lateral transfers, both from one two-year school to another and from one four-year school to another. It also includes many reverse transfers, in which students move from four-year to two-year schools.

One of the crucial things for you to keep in mind is that four-year schools don't simply accept transfer students; they need them. There is a lot of attrition among students entering community colleges and four-year schools. In the case of four-year schools, attrition takes the form of reverse transfers as well as dropping out of school altogether.

This means that virtually all four-year schools seek qualified transfer students—from other four-year schools or from community colleges—to bolster their higher-year enrollments and their degree completion rates. Community college students are an attractive choice, because they have already survived that early attrition period and have proven that they can succeed in college. Many have already completed an associate's degree. This is why transfers from community colleges complete their bachelor's degrees at a higher rate than students who enter the same four-year schools as freshmen.

Fernando Schiefelbein started his higher education at Coastal Carolina Community College in Jacksonville, North Carolina, while he was still a junior in high school. He began his first year at Coastal with an entire semester worth of credits.

Eventually he transferred to the University of North Carolina, where he graduated *magna cum laude* with a bachelor's degree in applied mathematics and went on to receive his master's degree. The institution that gave him his first taste of higher education is now his employer. He teaches statistics and calculus at Coastal. He realizes the true value of a community college education when counseling students about possible careers. "The classes are smaller and the faculty prepares students for either jobs or university courses. I didn't realize it when I was a student, but I now know how valuable my experience was at Coastal and how it shaped who I am today," he says.

Additionally, both public and private four-year schools need and want community college student transfers in order to meet diversity goals. This is because minorities make up a much higher proportion of two-year student bodies than four-year student bodies.

Kwame Walker grew up in the projects of Orlando, Florida. He received a scholarship to Valencia College in Orlando, but first had to take remedial math and reading before progressing to college level work. Although he struggled at first, he went on to graduate with an associate degree with a 3.0 GPA. He is now attending the University of Central Florida and volunteers to speak to at-risk kids in the Orange County Public School System. "If it weren't for Valencia, I would either be dead or in jail," he says.

Last, public four-year colleges and universities in many states need community college transfers so they can meet bachelor's degree attainment goals. A growing number of states have been mandating such goals, and even making them a basis for their higher education funding. As a result, it is not uncommon for community college transfers to make up 20 to 30 percent of the student body at public four-year schools.

All of these factors benefit transfer students and prospective transfer students. Because they need each other to serve upward-bound, lateral, and reverse transfers, community colleges and public four-year schools in every state are working together more closely than ever before. State higher education boards are devoting more attention to transfer processes. The many private four-year schools that accept transfers from within their own states and out of state are also working to improve their transfer acceptance processes.

As a result, transfer requirements and procedures have become much clearer and more streamlined over recent years. There are also many more support structures for prospective transfer students than ever before. However, you need to understand that even the best-case scenario will require you to do a lot more than just declare a desire to transfer in order to make it happen. If you want to transfer from community college to a bachelor's degree program—and make the transfer work for you—you will have to surmount a number of obstacles along the way.

The biggest problem is figuring out what course credits you can transfer. In response, many states have mandated that bachelor's degree programs at all of their four-year public colleges and universities adopt the same core requirements for lower-division general education courses and prerequisite courses for different majors. However, there is still plenty of variation in what four-year schools and their major programs are looking for and will accept. And if you change your major, you may have to satisfy a much different set of requirements than you initially thought.

There are also financial aid issues to consider. Financial aid continuity between two-year and four-year schools is not automatic, and the amount of financial aid may not always increase as it should.

You also have to expect and be able to handle a degree of "transfer shock." You'll be transitioning to a new school with an unfamiliar pace, academic style, and campus and social environment; you shouldn't underestimate the difficulty of adjusting to these changes.

The bottom line is that you will have to be more focused, disciplined, and active on your own behalf than the typical student who enters a bachelor's degree program in the first year. However, good planning and follow-through will help you succeed—and allow you to reap major rewards. You'll enjoy substantial tangible rewards in money saved and degree(s) earned. You'll also reap significant intangible rewards such as increased confidence and personal skills as you accomplish your academic goals and prepare yourself for a good career.

Now let's look at the transfer process in some detail, beginning with a brief vocabulary lesson.

Transfer Terminology

You need to know a few essential terms to navigate the transfer process:

- *Transfer* means moving your completed course work from one institution to another.
- *Transfer credit* means that an institution other than the one where you completed the work will accept it. You usually

have to earn a C grade or better for one of your courses to qualify for transfer credit.

- *Block credit transfer* means that you do not have to get your credits approved course by course. Instead, the courses in a block transfer are accepted to satisfy a whole category of requirements, such as lower-division general education requirements or prerequisites for a major.

- The *sending institution* is the institution you attend before transferring. It is where you complete course work that you then apply to a program at another institution.

- The *receiving institution* is the institution you attend after transferring. Receiving institutions can grant transfer credits to individual courses or to entire certificate and degree programs.

- The *residency requirement* is the percentage of courses or number of credit hours you have to complete at the receiving institution before it will grant you a certificate or degree. The residency requirement for bachelor's degree programs is two academic years at most schools, but it is only one academic year at some schools.

- *Articulation* refers to the institutional or statewide policies and structures for transferring course credit. This usage comes from a secondary meaning of the word *articulation*, which the *American Heritage Dictionary* defines as "a jointing together" or "the method or manner of jointing." If you ever take an anatomy class, you will learn about the articulation, or jointing together, of the bones of the skeleton.

- *Articulation and transfer agreements* stipulate which courses students can apply to meet a four-year school's lower-division general education requirements or fulfill the prerequisites for a specific major. These agreements may be only between certain two-year and four-year schools, public or private, that have formed a unique transfer partnership. Or they may include all of a state's public two-year and four-year schools.

Planning to Transfer

The sooner you start planning to transfer up from a community college to complete your bachelor's degree, the better. It's a good idea to begin your planning in high school, if possible. In effect you'll be choosing both a community college and a target four-year school or group of four-year schools.

Many students, especially those of you who live in major metropolitan areas, may have a choice of community colleges. If this is the case, one of your selection criteria should be the community college's transfer advising and its transfer agreements with both in-state and out-of-state four-year schools. Let the admissions office know that you're interested in transferring to earn a bachelor's degree, and ask if you can speak to a transfer advisor. Almost every community college has transfer advisors. At many community colleges you will also be able to talk to transfer advisors from four-year schools who either visit the campus regularly or have a permanent office there.

Transfer advisors can tell you about the articulation and transfer agreements that are in place between the community college and specific four-year schools or in your state generally. They can also inform you about general education and major preparation requirements in the field(s) of study you find most interesting.

The websites of community colleges, four-year schools, and state education boards are also important sources of information. For example, the state of Indiana now has a Transfer Indiana program with a website at www.TransferIN.net. It's a one-stop shop for anything and everything to do with transferring between colleges and universities in Indiana. Most states have similar websites, and those that don't are catching up fast.

After you enroll at community college, be sure to talk to your academic advisor about transferring. He or she will be able to help you choose the courses that will maximize your transfer potential and your ability to complete your bachelor's degree after you transfer. Discuss your transfer plans and progress with both your academic advisor and transfer advisor at least once a semester to make sure you are on track to your goal.

In order to transfer smoothly to a bachelor's degree program, you'll need to take a challenging course load in community college. As your community college academic and transfer advisors will surely tell you, this will improve your chances of transferring to a good four-year school. Even if you are not planning on a STEM-related major, it is probably to your advantage to take math and lab science courses that qualify for credit toward a bachelor's degree. And keep in mind that the grade you earn isn't the only factor. Getting a B in a rigorous course will impress a four-year school much more than getting an A in an easy course. (The same thinking applies to your high school course load, as I'll explain in Chapter 8, "What You Should Do to Prepare for College-Level Work if You Are Now in High School.")

If you have enrolled at community college knowing that you want to transfer but without having done this preliminary research, don't wait any longer. Talk to your academic advisor about transferring and meet with a transfer advisor during your first semester. After that, make regular appointments with both advisors to discuss transferring.

Of course, it may take a semester or longer before you're even aware that you want to transfer. You might enter college without any definite academic interest, and then get excited enough by one of your courses to want to major in that field and progress to a bachelor's degree. Or you might have some other experience that changes your sense of yourself or your life plans. These kinds of events are part of life, and part of higher education. You can't arrange everything in advance, and you've always got to stay open to new possibilities.

That said, the less time you have to get all your ducks in a row, the more stressful the transfer process will be. So procrastinate as little as possible!

The Best Time to Transfer

It's never too early to start planning to transfer. However, the ideal time for the transfer itself to occur is usually after you complete an associate's degree. The associate's degree is a valuable credential in its own right, especially in a STEM or health care–related field, as I explained in Chapter 4. Having an associate's degree will also make it much more likely that you can enter a bachelor's degree program as a junior. (It's actually a guarantee in some states, as I explain in the "What To Look for in a Transfer Program" section.)

Some students transfer after only one year at community college. Although this may work out for you, there is a downside to consider. Unless you can also transfer dual credits you earned in high school, this approach doesn't maximize community college's cost-saving and credit-earning potential. If you enter a four-year school with only one or two semesters' worth of transferable credits, you'll wind up paying almost as much to earn your bachelor's degree as if you started at the four-year school as a freshman.

And if you don't take a challenging enough course load, you could also wind up with too few credits to apply to your bachelor's degree and/or your major requirements—even after two years in community college. This might also happen is if you change majors, or fail to declare one, during your time at community college.

Whether or not you need more than a semester to find your footing as a college student—or settle on the major that is best for you—is a part of life you can't necessarily control. And it doesn't say anything one way or the other about your abilities or potential. However, there is no point in wasting time, either, and floating along is generally not a good strategy. You'll likely do best if you think hard about what you want to do in life, and take advantage of the counsel you can get from family members, teachers, advisors, and other mentors.

It may sound crazy, but you can also have too many credits when you transfer. This can occur as the result of a significant new trend in how states are funding their public colleges and universities. To encourage timely degree completion and hold down costs, many states are cutting the number of "excess credit hours"—those beyond the number needed to complete a degree—that they will automatically fund. For example, Texas cut the number of excess credit hours it will fund per student from 45 to 30 in 2005. Other states have made or are contemplating similar cuts.

If you come out of community college with a large number of credits that you cannot apply to your bachelor's degree, you can easily find yourself over the limit of what your state will fund. When you then have to take additional courses to meet your degree or major requirements, the four-year school may be able to charge you out-of-state tuition for those courses even if you're an in-state student, because it's not getting the usual funding from the state.

Finally, you can become ineligible for some financial aid by transferring too late in your college career. If you are enrolled at community college part time, you must remember that there is a nine-year maximum for Pell Grant eligibility (see Chapter 3, "Scholarships and Financial Aid"). The clock on that nine-year period starts ticking when you begin your postsecondary education.

What to Look for in a Transfer Program

Above all else, transfer programs should provide structured academic pathways from the community college to four-year schools and bachelor's degree programs in specific majors. These pathways should include transfer admission guarantees, assuming you maintain adequate grades. Although transfer admission guarantees often do not include admission into specific major programs, they do ensure that you will definitely gain admission to one of your state's public four-year colleges or universities—if you meet all the requirements. They will also make certain that your community college courses get you maximum credit toward your bachelor's degree.

The University of California and California State University systems both have transfer admission guarantees for students at California's public community colleges. The City University of New York (CUNY) system, Colorado, Florida, Hawaii, New Hampshire, and Virginia also have transfer admission guarantees for community college students. Florida has the most comprehensive transfer admission guarantee policy of any state, and is the only one to mandate that in-state students who earn an associate's degree at one of the state's public community colleges will gain admission to one of its public four-year schools as juniors.

A more common policy is that a state's public four-year colleges and universities give preference to transfer students from the same state's public community colleges. As a result of such a mandate in the California Master Plan for Higher Education, 90 percent of transfer acceptances at University of California and California State University campuses go to graduates of California community colleges.

In addition to statewide transfer admission guarantees and preferences, you should ask transfer advisors about your community college's individual articulation and transfer agreements with four-year colleges and universities. Ivy Tech, for example, has articulation and transfer agreements with 34 public and private Indiana four-year schools, including the flagship campuses of the Indiana University and Purdue University systems, and four out-of-state schools. Some of our transfer programs with four-year schools in Indiana are open to students at any of Ivy Tech's 30 campuses across the state. Others link particular Ivy Tech campuses and public four-year schools that are in close proximity to each other. We also have articulation and transfer agreements for online bachelor's degree programs at Western Governors University and Franklin University of Ohio.

Renowned international nonprofit organization the Aspen Institute, a Washington, D.C.–based think tank and policy group, has recognized Santa Barbara Community College in Santa Barbara, California, as a national leader in transfer programs. Through its "Express to Transfer" program, Santa Barbara Community College has over 30 articulation and transfer agreements with both in-state and out-of-state schools.

A number of private four-year colleges and universities have programs for transfer students from community colleges. For example, Georgetown University works with selected community colleges for transfers through its Preferred Consideration Program. Wheaton College in Massachusetts also has partnerships with selected community colleges. And New York University's Community College Transfer Opportunity Program has partnered with 13 community colleges in the New York metropolitan area to identify candidates for scholarships to two of the university's divisions: the Steinhardt School of Culture, Education, and Human Development, and the Paul McGhee Division of the NYU School of Continuing and Professional Studies.

Many other four-year colleges and universities have such programs. It's therefore always a good idea to ask the admissions offices and/or the transfer advisors at your target four-year schools about their partnerships with community colleges.

The most student-friendly and seamless transfer programs are those that offer *dual* or *concurrent* enrollment. These programs usually occur at a community college and a four-year school that are more or less in the same neighborhood, so that you can get back and forth between the two fairly easily. Dual or concurrent enrollment programs give you access to the four-year school's campus activities and student services from the first day of your studies at the community college. In some cases, you can even live in the four-year school's residence halls while doing your first two years of course work at the community college. You may also be able to take one or two courses a term at the four-year college. As long as you maintain the required grade average, which is usually a B, you are guaranteed admission to the four-year school after you complete your associate's degree at the community college.

Texas A&M University's flagship campus in College Station, Texas, and its close community college neighbor, Blinn College, launched such a program during the 1999–2000 academic year.

As the College Board describes it in a report on best practices in transfers from community colleges to four-year schools, "Texas A&M at College Station recruits most of its transfers from nearby Blinn College, a partnership that represents one of the first dual admission programs. Eligible students are admitted concurrently to Blinn College and Texas A&M. These students are allowed to complete up to six credits per semester at A&M and have access to all of A&M's campus programs and services. If they earn at least a B average at Blinn, they automatically transfer to A&M as juniors."

Iowa State University, located in Ames, Iowa, has an Admission Partnership Program that offers dual enrollment with several nearby community colleges, including Des Moines Community College, which is less than an hour's drive away. As Iowa State University Director of Admissions Marc Harding says, "Isn't it cool that you can be an Admission Partnership Program student taking courses at Des Moines Community College but living in our residence halls, so you can feel a part of the Iowa State community?"

Ivy Tech has a successful dual enrollment program with Indiana State University, Indiana Univeristy, Purdue University, Indiana University–Purdue University–Indianapolis (IUPUI), and Indiana University–Purdue University Fort Wayne (IPFW), among others.

A Jack Kent Cooke Foundation–sponsored program has enabled the University of North Carolina (UNC) to provide a dual enrollment program for students at several Raleigh-Durham area community colleges. Like the other such programs I've highlighted, the UNC program has strict academic standards—not every student transfers successfully. However, these programs have become benchmarks in community college to four-year school transfer because they offer such well-structured and seamless pathways for students' progress—if they are disciplined and dedicated enough.

Unfortunately, dual enrollment programs are not available in every state. California instituted a dual enrollment program in 2002–2003, only to eliminate it in 2004–2005 as part of a budget cut.

(See the "Additional Resources" Appendix for a list of dual enrollment programs around the country.)

Although they often seem necessary at the time, these kinds of
budget cuts are extremely shortsighted. There is no better investment
in economic growth than education. Investment in community
colleges has an especially impressive rate of return, as I've already
discussed in Chapter 2, "Affordable for All" (for more on this, see also
the "The Higher Education America Needs" Appendix).

Last, as you investigate transfer opportunities, you should look
for good transfer-student support services at the four-year school
(for more on this, see "Surviving Transfer Shock," below). Transfer
shock, which I mentioned at the beginning of this chapter,
can easily get you off track from completing your bachelor's
degree. Four-year schools used to assume that transfer students did
not need any targeted services after they arrived on campus.
Although they've now recognized transfer shock as a serious issue,
not every four-year school offers the support services that transfer
students need.

Surviving Transfer Shock

One of the big reasons for the success of dual enrollment programs
is that they significantly reduce transfer shock. Four-year schools'
academic styles, campus environments, and student bodies tend to
be quite different from those of community colleges. The pace can
also be faster, because many four-year schools have a quarter rather
than a semester system.

Lack of engagement in the four-year school's campus life is often
the biggest problem that community college transfers face. Dual
enrollment programs address this by giving community college
students the opportunity to take part in the four-year school's campus and student activities before they transfer. However, these programs can only accommodate a fraction of potential transfer
students. That's why it is important for states and four-year schools to

offer continuing support for transfer students from before they arrive on campus through the completion of their bachelor's degrees.

Good transfer-student support services include online resources and tools for managing the transfer process; required transfer-student orientation that is as comprehensive as what first-year students receive, but is transfer specific; help in securing adequate need-based financial aid and avoiding or bridging gaps between financial aid at the community college and four-year institution; merit-based transfer student scholarships; a transfer student center, whether or not as part of a general student center; and even on-campus childcare for transfer students with children.

Statewide transfer student support services mainly will be available to you online. For example, California has an extensive website, www.assist.org, to help students manage the transfer process. (The website's name is an acronym that stands for "Articulation System Stimulating Interinstitutional Student Transfer.") The site allows students to pick a California public community college and one of the state's public four-year schools, together with a specific major, and then instantly see the articulation and transfer agreement for the two schools and the major. Student transfer portals in other states, such as Indiana's www.transferIN.net (mentioned earlier in this chapter), have similar tools. The TransferIN.net website includes a course by course "Core Transfer Library," as well as specific resources for high school students, two-year and four-year college students, and guidance counselors.

UCLA's transfer-student support services illustrate the range of targeted services you can and should look for at four-year schools. UCLA's outreach process for transfer students begins with transfer peer mentoring in community college. Juniors and seniors at UCLA who themselves transferred from community college visit community colleges in the Los Angeles Basin to advise prospective transfer students. Incoming transfer students attend UCLA's residential, week-long "bridge" program in the summer before they enroll as juniors.

You may or may not need targeted transfer student services when you're completing your bachelor's degree. But it is good for them to be in place, if you do.

Financial aid continuity and an adequate amount of financial aid are crucial for practically every transfer student. For more on financial aid issues, see Chapter 3, "Scholarships and Financial Aid."

A Transfer Timeline and Checklist

Here is a combination timeline/checklist to help you plan and manage the transfer process:

- *During your senior year in high school or first semester at community college:* Investigate possible four-year schools and major programs; look for articulation and transfer agreements that fit your academic and career goals; contact your community college's transfer advisor; begin to keep a physical and/ or digital copy of the syllabus for each of your community college courses, so that you can regularly evaluate how many transferable credits you are earning.

- *During your second semester at community college:* Continue researching four-year schools and major programs, paying particular attention to any special requirements and deadlines; visit four-year school campuses if possible, and discuss your plans with their admissions offices and transfer student advisors; stay in touch with your community college's transfer advisor.

- *During your third semester at community college:* Investigate four-year school financial aid, including merit-based scholarships and need-based grants specifically for transfer students; secure letters of recommendation from community college professors and instructors; get your transcripts in order; continue to discuss your transfer plans with your academic advisor and transfer advisor.

- *During your fourth community college semester:* Submit your transfer applications and financial aid information to four-year schools.

Advance this timeline as needed to meet transfer requirements at the four-year school(s) where you are applying.

■ ■ ■

Community colleges offer two other great career track options in addition to transferring to complete a bachelor's degree: two-year associate's degrees and one-year professional certificates. We'll explore these options in the next chapter.

6

Two-Year Degrees and One-Year Professional Certificates

Gateway Credentials to Great Jobs and Careers

Who's Got the Time—or Money—to Go to College?

Many smart, hard-working people in this country believe they're about as likely to graduate college as they are to go to the moon. As I discussed in earlier chapters, most middle-income families cannot afford the four-year residential college experience. And most of the population as a whole cannot even afford to become full-time students. For millions of Americans, community colleges offer a better way.

While much of higher education still functions as it did a century ago, community colleges are reinventing themselves to meet the higher education needs of students from underserved communities and demographic groups of all ethnicities. We recognize that the traditional college structure doesn't work for millions of Americans, and we're moving quickly to put college credentials—and good jobs—within their reach. As one commentator puts it, community colleges are the "speedboats of higher education."[1] We're fast and nimble, and we can turn on a dime. And we're doing that in many ways, making the changes that are necessary to fit the times.

Today's college students are nothing like they used to be. Only 25 percent of them fit the ivory-tower stereotype and attend school full time at residential colleges. Indeed, about 40 percent are part-time students who are juggling jobs, families, and school.[2] Time is a precious resource for these students, and as research has proved, the longer it takes for them to get a degree, the less likely they are to get it.

Community colleges are aware of this fact. We're building fast and convenient programs for this new breed of students, and streamlining them to weed out nonessential course work. And we're not just taking out what today's students don't need; we're beefing up whatever directly moves them toward their ultimate goal—a good job. These programs take two forms: associate's degrees, which can be completed in two years of full-time study; and professional certificates, which can be completed in a few months to a little over a year.

Two-Years and a Career

In the discussion in Chapter 4 of STEM-related and health care–related careers, I highlighted a number of two-year degrees that offer a path to a great future. In the same chapter, I also noted the data showing that 31 percent of associate's degrees earn more than a bachelor's degree. That's a national figure. The situation in Indiana looks even better, thanks I believe to the quality of Ivy Tech's graduates. In 38 of Indiana's 92 counties, or 41 percent of the state, those with an associate's degree earn more than those with a recent bachelor's degree.

Here let me just mention a few more two-year degrees that lead to good careers. An associate's degree in business positions you for a starting salary of $49,400. An associate's degree in accounting commands a starting salary of $37,700. An associate's degree in nursing will credential you as a registered nurse, an occupation with a starting salary of $43,410 and median earnings of $60,000.

Associate's degrees in medical assisting, computer information systems or technology, and advanced manufacturing earn starting salaries of $39,570, $41,000, and $44,000, respectively.

Earning an associate's degree won't saddle you with debt. It will get you out into the workforce quickly, so that you can begin to advance in your career and life goals. It can command a starting salary better than many liberal arts bachelor's degrees, and give you upside potential beyond that, especially in STEM and health care occupations. And it is a credential you can use as a stepping-stone if you decide to go back to school for a bachelor's degree.

Now let's look at one-year certificates, which can really speed you into the workforce with skills that employers value.

Certificates: The Most Direct Way to the American Dream

The fastest courses of study in community colleges are called certificate programs. Students in these programs earn credentials that certify they have completed a discrete course of study. Thanks to concentrated, flexible schedules, these programs typically deliver high-demand skills and a credential in months, not years.

Complete College America, a Washington, D.C.—based advocacy group pushing to increase the number of college graduates in the United States, has concluded that certificate programs are an "underutilized strategy" and "the most direct way to get a college credential."[3] They are becoming a gateway to a good job and a better life for millions of Americans who once never could have gone to college.

Georgetown University's Anthony Carnevale, whose preeminent research in workforce development we looked at in Chapter 4, praises these certificate programs' efficiency. "There's very little general education associated with them," he says. "That is, you don't take history . . . [or] foreign language. You take whatever it is you need to know to do the work in your occupation. . . . You will need math in a lot of these occupations. But you won't get Algebra II [in certificate programs]; you'll get the math that's required to run the machines and do the work in your occupation. It's a very different kind of education."[4]

Certificate programs are growing in popularity. The most recent tally suggests that at least 750,000 certificates are awarded each year nationwide—roughly equal to the number of associate's degrees awarded. Certificates are the dominant community college credential in some states. For example, schools in Louisiana and Georgia award three times as many certificates as they do associate's degrees.[5]

The most popular certificate programs prepare students for jobs in health care, business, and technology. But the range of offerings is truly mind-boggling. Here at Ivy Tech, we offer more than 50 certificates that equip students to enter fields such as:

- medicine and health care
- business
- manufacturing
- computers and information technology
- public safety
- accounting
- education and youth counseling

Most of our programs are highly specialized. For instance, we have a short-term auto-repair program that specifically teaches individuals how to work on electric and hybrid cars. Another trains students in alternative-fuel systems. Yet another provides training in Java programming. And while our two-year and three-year nursing programs are extremely popular, we've also developed fast programs to train massage therapists and medical technicians.

Many of our newest certificate programs are part of the Ivy Institute of Technology, which offers accelerated programs that deliver credentials to students for rewarding jobs in one of six high-demand areas: machine tools; welding; heating, ventilating, and air conditioning (HVAC); automotive; mechatronics/advanced manufacturing; and office administration. Each program runs for just 30 weeks, with students meeting for six hours a day. If you go into one of these programs, you can be ready for the workforce in just eight months. The new Ivy Tech programs are closely modeled on the Tennessee Technology Centers, which I discuss later in this Chapter.

You'll find certificate programs in an amazing array of areas and fields at community colleges around the country. Community colleges are tailoring their programs to regional economies and industries in order to graduate students who can step right in, contribute to economic growth, and make a good living. After witnessing the growth of wind farms in the heartland states, Mitchell Technical Institute in South Dakota started one of the country's first programs to train wind-turbine technicians. In addition to a two-year associate's degree, it offers a one-year certificate that qualifies students for work in the field, climbing turbines and building and repairing them. The school even has its own wind turbine.[6]

The Road to a Very Good Life: The One-Year Certificate

So how long do you need to go to school? Some programs run less than a year and will land you a great job. Training to become a Cisco Systems technician typically runs less than a year, yet "it's the gold standard in information-technology certificates," says Josh Wynder, director of the College Excellence Program at the Aspen Institute.

In general, however, a certificate program of at least a year is likelier to provide the high-demand skills that will gain you entry into a well-paid occupation. Research indicates that these somewhat longer programs have the biggest payoff for students. According to a study by Complete College America, "Certificates of one year or more are consistently linked to increased earnings."

The study cites findings from Kentucky that show the average income for people who earned certificates of at least a year in duration was nearly the same as what individuals with associate's degrees earned.

Consider the case of Tricia Jenkins, who graduated in 2010 with a certificate in court reporting from Alvin Community College in Alvin, Texas, and now makes $78,800 as a court reporter for Merrill Legal Solutions in Houston. "My certification in court reporting cost $9,000 and I paid back my loan during my first three months of employment," she says.

She plans to take additional courses at Alvin to become a certified real-time reporter, which will enable her to produce simultaneous translation and display of live proceedings utilizing computer-aided transcription. This will also guarantee her a higher salary. "Court reporting is a fabulous, interesting job. Every day is different whether in the courts at depositions. I would recommend it to anyone," she notes.

One-year programs also often have lower dropout rates than longer programs, in part because many are "built for completion" and stripped of all but the requirements essential for you to get the job you want. Of course, not all one-year certificate programs deliver. You want a high-quality program that has the following ingredients:

- *Block scheduling.* Colleges should recognize that students with jobs or children need a predictable class schedule, with course work concentrated in a single block of time during the day or week. Random class schedules, in which course times are scattered across different periods throughout the week, are the enemy of anyone trying to juggle their education with real life. Studies show that students pursuing a degree often have to give up when schedule conflicts keep them from enrolling in required classes.

- *Remediation work is part of the program, not a barrier to starting.* Community colleges refer to courses designed to help you prepare to do college-level work as remediation, or remedial classes. Remediation can be a significant obstacle on the route to a credential. For example, while many students arrive at Ivy Tech's doors not quite ready for college-level work, we don't shuttle them into remediation tracks, forcing them to wait to start their industry-related studies until they finish courses in basic skills. Instead, we fold basic-skills preparation into every specialty program and waive skills requirements when students demonstrate competency. For more on remediation, see Chapter 10, "The Placement Tests That Determine Where You Start in College."

- *The curriculum is "built for completion."* Rather than let students pick and choose what courses to take en route to a degree, community colleges increasingly require students to take an established set of courses. This program of study is carefully selected to include everything the students need in their chosen field, but nothing else—all the better to speed them along the way. Such programs often give students the chance to progress when they demonstrate competency in a set of skills. In other words, once you've learned something, you don't waste time sitting in class waiting for the course to finish.

- *Curriculum and faculty are closely tied to local employers and employment needs.* The best community colleges know what the local economy and job market need. They hire teachers from community businesses, partner with companies big and small, and analyze what industries will be booming in the coming years.

- *There are plenty of opportunities for hands-on training.* Whether you're training to be a nurse, a biotech engineer, or a massage therapist, the best teacher is experience. Good programs put students in the field as interns or apprentices to enable them to learn by doing the job for which they're training. Some go to great lengths to provide hands-on experience. South Dakota's Lake Area Technical Institute, for example, has its airplane mechanic students work on a FedEx jet that was recently retired from service.

- *Good pass rates on certification tests.* After you earn a professional certificate from a community college, you usually also have to pass an industry- or state-administered certification test. You can gauge the quality of a certificate program by how many students who earn certificates also pass their certification tests. A low pass rate means the program isn't rigorous enough to do you much good in the job market. High-quality programs have pass rates of at least 75 percent.
- *Good job placement rates.* The ultimate test of a certificate program is how many students get jobs in that field. High-quality programs have job placement rates of at least 75 percent.

Tennessee Tech: Providing a Career in a Year

Many experts point to the one-year certificate programs at the 27 Tennessee Technology Centers as among the best in the country. Located throughout the state, these centers got their start in the 1960s as conventional vocational educational schools. They now stand as a model of how to deliver education that is tailored to so-called nontraditional students: people past traditional college age who are seeking to change careers and enhance their opportunities in the job market. Their students' average age is 32, and most come from low-income families—half are from households with annual earnings of $12,000 or less.

Tuition is low; it's typically $2,400 for a year, and $4,000 at most for programs lasting more than a year. The majority of students find scholarships and federal aid cover all their direct education costs and even some of their indirect costs, such as travel and childcare.

Each of the 27 Tennessee Technology Centers focuses on the mission of workforce training in its own region of the state. Altogether they offer more than 50 certificate programs, with some preparing students in very specific skills—masonry, computer-based graphic design, aircraft mechanics, cardiovascular sonography, and much more. There's no push for liberal arts here—the centers leave the traditional academic fields to the state's 13 other community colleges because they want streamlined programs focused solely on teaching skills that are valuable in the workplace. Their programs are about education *and* jobs—a combination you won't find at many four-year colleges. Center leaders say their programs are aimed to provide "a career in a year." The Nashville Center's motto is "Real Skills for Real Jobs."

The centers' program structure is remarkable. Center leaders recognize that the typical college format—with classes scheduled at random times—can wreak havoc on the average adult's work life or childcare arrangements. Such unpredictability makes it nearly impossible for career-changing students to go to school full time. Accordingly, most of Tennessee's programs run a block schedule, with classes starting at 7:30 or 8:00 AM and running to 2:30 or 3:00 PM, which matches most K–12 schedules. This concentration of course work makes it possible for students to plan their lives outside the classroom and meet their job and childcare commitments.

The tech centers also design their programs in a way that allows students to advance at their own pace. Everything is competency-based; once you demonstrate a skill, you move on to the next rung. There is no waiting around for others in your class to catch up, and there is no problem if you need to proceed at a slower pace because of job or home commitments or some other factor. The same goes for any remedial work you may need in specialty-related math or another area. This work takes place concurrently with training in the job specialty, so it doesn't slow down students en route to getting the certificate.

The end result is terrific. "Nobody does it as well as the Tennessee Tech Centers," says Tom Sugar of Complete College America.

"They've been doing it for a long time, so there's a track record to follow."

Student performance vouches for the quality of education at the centers. In 2008, 96 percent of students who sat for a licensure test in such fields as nursing or welding passed on the first try. Overall, three-quarters of the students who enroll in a Tennessee Tech program complete their certificate or degree. By comparison, only 57 percent of students at the state's four-year schools graduate on time.

Last, the centers also do incredibly well on the ultimate measure of their training: job placement. Eighty-five percent of their graduates get a job in their desired field. With some programs, the results are even more impressive. In one recent year, every student who trained in cardiovascular sonography or nuclear medicine was placed after graduation. And 98 percent of students in the paramedics program found jobs as paramedics.

The owner of a parts-machining company told a researcher that tech-center graduates often have the same skills as workers with two or three years of experience. "They're that well trained and ready to work," he said. Carol Puryear, director of the Tech Center at Murfreesboro, agrees: "Students walk out of here and they are able to have a very good life, with or without further education."[7]

Why a Community College Certificate Might Earn You a Bigger Salary

Although I've already discussed this point in Chapter 4, some of you may still be wondering whether earning a community college certificate will enable you to earn enough to sustain a family and provide them with a good quality of life.

According to the Final Four Syndrome, the road to the American dream runs almost exclusively through four-year schools and their grassy campuses filled with tweed-blazer-wearing professors. But as we saw in Chapters 1 to 4, that syndrome is out of touch with two parallel current realities: the runaway cost of the four-year residential college experience, and the skills that employers are really seeking—and will pay top dollar to get.

Georgetown University labor economist Anthony Carnevale, whose research I cited in Chapter 4, and other workforce researchers have found that short-term credentials—usually from programs lasting one to two years—are a new, perhaps better choice for many Americans. According to the data, nearly a third of people with one- and two-year credentials earn more than people with bachelor's degrees.[8]

Although that might seem counterintuitive, the trend reflects changes in our country's economy. As I described in Chapter 4, career fields involving science and technology are exploding at the same time the availability of qualified workers is shrinking. This imbalance means that with a certificate in the right field, you can command more money with your community-college certificate than someone with a four-year degree.

I've emphasized that where you study is much less important than what you study. It's also true that compared to many liberal arts majors, as *Washington Post* education writer Daniel de Vise puts it, "It doesn't matter how long you have studied; it matters what you study."[9]

A one-year certificate in the right field can indeed position you to have a great life, even if you don't add further higher education credentials. But you also should never forget that your first choice of a higher education credential does not put a ceiling on your career possibilities. To the contrary, it puts a floor under you and enables you to reach higher. And one-year certificates can be a great place to start.

■ ■ ■

Now that we've explored the range of valuable higher education credentials you can achieve at community college, let's look at an option that will increasingly be part of every higher education experience: online learning.

7 On Campus or Online?

Do you want to take courses on your own schedule, not the school's or the teacher's? Do you like the idea of never having to travel to campus, yet at the same time never having to miss a class, an instructor's office hours, collaboration on group projects and "study jams" with classmates, or even the lab components of science courses? Do you want to be able to do all these things from your home or office, or while you're traveling? And do you want to do your course work at your own pace and in your own style? Do you picture yourself "attending" class in your pajamas? Or do you imagine yourself managing to squeeze in lectures, reading, and assignments at night or on weekends, whenever there is time to spare from work and family tasks?

That's all part of the promise of online learning, and to a great extent it's a reality that delivers enormous financial benefit and convenience, in the form of savings in travel time and cost, to hundreds of thousands of students. As I'll explain, online learning is not for everyone in every situation. However, if it suits your personal characteristics and circumstances, it can be a terrific way for you to get some, or perhaps all, of the higher education you need in order to achieve your career and life plans.

Online learning, also known as distance learning or distance education, has been one of the most significant developments in education over the past 30 years. And community colleges have been at the forefront of this development. Rio Salado College, one of 10 community colleges in the Maricopa County Community College District, which serves the greater Phoenix, Arizona, area, was founded as an online institution in 1978. Today Rio Salado is the country's second largest online public community college, with over 43,000 unduplicated students taking at least one of its more than 640 online courses.

Ivy Tech is the largest online public community college, thanks to our being a statewide, singly accredited institution with 30 campuses throughout Indiana, but also thanks to our early, continuing leadership in developing online higher education offerings. In 1995, Ivy Tech offered its first online credit course in writing. In 1997, our Terre Haute campus launched the first accredited online programs in the nation for two-year colleges, with programs in accounting, design, and office administration. We had a total of 223 online students in the first semester of these three programs, and our growth in online education since then has been dramatic.

In the 2010–2011 academic year, we had 79,123 unduplicated online students in 300 credit-earning online courses. Both the number of students and the total courses offered are increasing every semester. We're steadily adding online courses across the full range of academic and career disciplines. We also offer programs that are wholly or mostly online in 13 subject areas: accounting, business administration, computer information systems, criminal justice, design technology, early childhood education (with practicum components done offline), general studies, human services (again, with a few components such as clinical internships done offline), information security, library technology, manufacturing production and operations, office administration, and paralegal studies. All in all, 36 percent of Ivy Tech's students take online courses, and they average two online courses per semester.

In this chapter I'm going to draw on Ivy Tech's extensive, successful leadership in online learning. The chapter will portray online learning's many benefits and a few potential pitfalls, help you decide if it's right for you, and show you how to make the most of it.

■ ■ ■

Some community college students, especially younger ones coming straight from high school, consider online courses and think, "Great! I'll save lots of money and time by not having to get back and forth to school. I can find a part-time job and still go to school full time." For their part, older students with children also often think, "I won't have to worry about arranging or paying for childcare."

These time- and money-saving aspects of online education are genuine. But students who focus solely on the convenience of online courses tend to be the ones who wind up struggling in them. Mostly this is because they assume the course work itself is somehow going to be easier in an online course as opposed to an on-campus one.

That's a big mistake. Online courses are just as rigorous as those offered on campus (and don't forget, community college courses are just as rigorous as those at four-year schools). As we'll see below, online courses frequently require more work of various kinds—readings, exams, term papers, individual and group projects—than on-campus courses do. Dr. Paul Amador, director of advising at Ivy Tech's Bloomington campus, says, "Students who are focused on convenience see doing courses online as a solution, but it can turn out to be a hindrance if they assume that the courses are going to be easy just because they're online. That isn't the case at all."

On the other hand, many students avoid online courses because they're afraid they might not be as comprehensive and effective as traditional, on-campus courses. Thinking this way also represents a big mistake—in the form of a missed opportunity. Thanks to robust digital tools and rapidly advancing course management software and systems, online courses can be every bit as comprehensive in content, as varied in approach, and—most important—as effective as on-campus courses are.

In fact, online courses are well on the way to becoming an equal partner with on-campus courses in college curricula. Although online courses first appeared prominently in higher education at public community colleges, and then at for-profit schools, they have now become an important component of the curriculum at many traditional four-year schools, as well.

Wherever you get your higher education in the years ahead, online courses will be an important part of the picture. Instead of just a brick-and-mortar model for higher education, there are now two additional models: brick and click, for a combination of on-campus and online learning; and click only, for completely online learning in a course or an entire program of courses. These are not mutually exclusive options, but rather are complementary ones that instructors and students can mix and match to suit course and program goals.

Cost is driving this trend. As we saw earlier in the book, the economy needs increasing numbers of better-educated, more highly credentialed workers in every industry. This is sending more and more students into higher education, whether they come straight out of high school or after some time in the workforce. Yet frozen or decreasing higher education budgets make it impossible to build enough physical facilities to accommodate these skyrocketing enrollments. Online education is essential to bridge this gap.

However, it's not just a matter of cost. The existing capabilities of online learning technology already make online courses a rich adjunct or alternative to on-campus courses. And these capabilities are expanding quickly as the technology advances and evolves.

■ ■ ■

Whether online courses will be effective for you depends on your personal characteristics, temperament, and learning style. Students who do well in online courses can accurately describe themselves as follows:

- "I enjoy learning independently, but am comfortable asking an instructor for help if I don't understand something."
- "I am organized and maintain a schedule of all the things I need to get done. I don't generally need to be reminded to complete things on time or even a little early."
- "I am comfortable using a computer and the Internet to do things like viewing a web page, sending and reading e-mail, typing papers in a word processing program, and finding information on the Internet."
- "I learn well from reading and reflecting on what I have read. I don't need to listen to a lecture to help me understand course content."
- "I have at least ten hours a week to devote to each course I am taking and can make more time if needed."

How about you? Can you describe yourself in these ways? Don't take these questions lightly. To quote Ivy Tech's Dr. Paul Amador again, "Students like the idea of not paying for gas for their car or other transportation to and from school. They like not having to arrange or pay for childcare. But human nature is such that it is much easier to motivate ourselves to do something if we have to go someplace special to do it. The idea that they don't have to show up in person to talk to an instructor or hand in their work sounds very good to some students on the surface. But the computer's not going to pop up and say, 'Hey, did you get that assignment done?' You have to have a lot of extra motivation and discipline to get online and do your work when nobody is watching you or checking up on you."

That said, if you do have the motivation and discipline for online courses, they can be highly effective for you. With that in mind, you need to know that online courses come in a variety of forms. The main types are:

- Online only
- Videoconferencing
- Video streaming
- Video and online
- Hybrid (online and face to face)

These categories are based on standards defined by the Sloan Consortium, an effort of the Sloan Foundation, and represent what you will find at two- and four-year schools across the country.

As the name implies, *online-only courses* (often just referred to as *Internet courses*) take place entirely, or almost entirely, online. To qualify as "online only," according to the Sloan Consortium's definitions, a course's offerings must be at least 80 percent online. The only time a student may need to go to a campus or testing center is to take a proctored exam once or twice a semester. But in many online courses all exams and other course requirements can be done online from wherever students happen to be.

Online-only courses are asynchronous, meaning you're not bound by a set daily clock and weekly calendar. Instead, you can access the lectures and other content in an online-only course, and complete and submit assignments, whenever you want, so long as you keep pace with the requirements of the course syllabus. If you complete readings and other assignments ahead of the syllabus schedule, you can move ahead at a faster pace. Online-only courses may include opportunities for participating in online office hours, chats, or other "real-time" presentations. However, these additional activities will be optional, rather than required.

Videoconferencing courses use Internet protocol video to link students and instructors in different locations. For this sort of course, you will need to travel to a campus facility or a designated learning center. The class will meet at a specific day and time each week, and you will be able to interact with the instructor using a live audio and video feed. This is very much like a regular on-campus course, except that you might not even be in the same city as the instructor.

Courses that use *video streaming* (also called *synchronous online video*) enable you to view the course content from any location where you have a high-speed (cable modem, DSL, or higher) Internet connection. Each course session is basically a live webcast. You will need to have your own webcam and microphone that connect to, or are integral to, your computer, so that you can talk to your instructor and the other students in the class. These classes still meet at a set day and time each week, but give you the added convenience of being able to participate in the class from any location that has high-speed Internet access, a webcam, and a microphone. There may also be supplemental online content that students can access and review whenever they want. However, the majority of the course content will be delivered via real-time webcasts.

Video and online courses mix video and online learning, so students will need to feel comfortable using both methods of learning.

Hybrid courses combine traditional classroom instruction with online learning. Students in a hybrid class go to campus to participate in classroom and/or laboratory activities. They use the Internet to review content on the web, complete assignments and submit them online, and participate in online discussions and other online learning activities. In contrast to online-only courses, the online discussions and other real-time online components of a hybrid course will likely be required rather than optional. If you are interested in trying an online class, but aren't sure if it will be right for you, taking a hybrid course first is a good way to start.

As you can see from these descriptions, you will still need your own computer and high-speed Internet access, even if the course has a significant on-campus component. The current technical requirements for a good online learning experience are:

- Desktop, laptop, or tablet computer with a 1 GHz or faster central processing unit and 256 MB of random access memory (512 MB strongly suggested)
- Broadband Internet access
- Windows XP or later or Mac OS X 10.6 Snow Leopard (earlier versions of Mac OS X and Linux/Unix OS are not suitable for all online learning applications, but if you have a Mac you can get software that will let you work in Windows mode)
- CD-ROM drive (you may also need a DVD drive in some courses)
- Sound card, microphone, and speakers or headphones
- Video card and monitor capable of displaying at least 16-bit color (thousands of colors)

Students sometimes think they will be able to succeed in an online course by using the computers in a public library, a local school computer lab, or some other setting outside their own homes. In practice this usually doesn't work out well. As you take an online course, you are going to want to hop on and off the Internet to check information, download something, or perform some other task. Having access to a computer only on somebody else's terms probably won't cut it.

Likewise, students sometimes think that they can get by with 56K dial-up access to the Internet. Although this can be (barely) adequate in online-only courses, it will likely be a frustrating experience. And in the other types of online courses, for which you must be able to participate in chats and other online activities in real time, broadband Internet access is an absolute must. Many people cannot afford broadband access, and in many rural areas of the country, including parts of Indiana, broadband is not available at any price. Approximately 40 percent of the U.S. population lacks broadband access either because the cost is too great or the service is not offered where they live.

You need to be computer savvy to handle an online course. Depending on their backgrounds, many students still arrive at college without any significant computer experience. If you have your own computer and broadband access, you should be able to acquire the computer skills you need fairly quickly. However, you should fill in those gaps before you start taking online courses.

At Ivy Tech we use an online self-assessment tool called Smarter-Measure. Using this tool, students who aren't sure about their computer savvy can find out in 45 minutes whether they are ready to deal with the computer-related tasks they'll encounter in online courses. For those who aren't ready, there are computer-skills courses on campus that will quickly help them get up to speed.

We've found that there is a direct positive correlation between Ivy Tech students' taking a brief orientation course in online learning and their ability to complete online courses successfully. Community colleges around the country are seeing the same pattern. Through SmarterMeasure or similar tools and computer-skills courses, community colleges are working diligently to improve student readiness for online learning. And these efforts are paying off in the form of increasing rates of timely certificate and degree completion.

■ ■ ■

Let's assume you've got the personal characteristics and technical wherewithal—the motivation and discipline, the computer technology and savvy, and the broadband access—that online courses require. What will the experience of an online course be like? That depends to a large extent on the rapid evolution of course management software and systems. Ivy Tech and many other colleges, both two- and four-year schools, use the Blackboard course management system. There are other course management systems (they are also known as learning management systems), but Blackboard is far and away the market leader, and it is very popular with both Ivy Tech faculty and students.

Course management software programs have become highly sophisticated in recent years. Instructors can use these programs to incorporate a vast array of media and other elements into their courses (text materials; "canned" audio, video, and still images; and real-time presentations, discussions, and collaboration sessions), disseminate grades, and meet with students individually or in groups. Students can use the same tools to incorporate a similarly wide range of materials and activities into their assignments and studies.

Blackboard and other course management programs feature instant messaging tools for contacts between instructors and students, and provide instant links to resources such as online library searches or the campus bookstore. They are also seamlessly integrated with the latest social media, making it easy to create online communities that are course or program specific. Blogs, tweets, podcasts, webcasts, online chats, discussion boards, and virtual study jams are all part of the mix that is possible with today's course management tools.

Because of these capabilities, Blackboard has become an integral part of both on-campus and online courses at Ivy Tech. Faculty and students alike have embraced Blackboard for web management and web enhancement of on-campus courses. Similar developments are occurring at two- and four-year schools everywhere, whether with Blackboard or another learning management system. As I wrote earlier, online learning tools will soon be part of every higher education experience.

■ ■ ■

I can't think of a better example of the benefits that online education offers than the experience of Ivy Tech student Kimberly Wheeler Butts. Kim was a 30-year-old divorced mother of five children (nine, six, five, four, and three years old) when she started studying for an associate's degree in business administration at Ivy Tech's Richmond campus in May 2004.

Describing the situation, Kim told me, "I went through the tears and the pity party. I had one semester of college and worked as a graphic artist before I got married and started having children. Being out of the workforce for over 10 years and not having a college credential, I figured no one would ever hire me. But I went to Ivy Tech–Richmond and a wonderful counselor there, Stephanie Alexander, told me, 'First we have to educate you to make people want to hire you.'"

Although Kim had some childcare help from her own mother, her family commitments and finances meant she had to go to school part time and work part time. Just after she enrolled at Ivy Tech she saw an ad for a temporary part-time job in the Richmond campus's financial aid office. Kim was one of 30 applicants for what was only supposed to be a two-month position. Her can-do spirit not only won her the job, but her performance in it convinced Ivy Tech to hire her on a permanent part-time basis.

For the first two years, Kim took only on-campus courses. Kim says, "I'm a parent first, and my kids really needed me to be around more. So with a lot of trepidation, because I didn't know what to expect, I tried an online course. Now you couldn't pay me to take a course that only meets in a physical classroom. Online classes gave me the flexibility I needed, and saved me a lot of money on gas and childcare on days when my mom couldn't help with that."

As I noted above, online classes are just as rigorous as on-campus classes, and sometimes are even more demanding. Kim found that to be true. "My experience is that instructors give more homework and assign more reading in online courses, because you're not sitting in front of them in a lecture hall every week and they want to make sure you're learning what you should. And some things are just plain harder online than offline. If you're doing a virtual lab in an online biology class, it's a lot different from actually dissecting a frog with a lab partner. It's more difficult because you have to think and read a lot more into it. You have to be more disciplined and motivated in online classes. You have to have that want and need to learn. But if you do, online courses are great and they're just so convenient. That's why I switched to all online courses."

The course management software I've been talking about played a big role in Kim's success in online courses. She says, "In every online class, I used Blackboard to connect with other students and form Facebook groups for just our class. Bunches of us regularly got together online to study, compare notes, and cheer each other on as we did our writing and other assignments. And Blackboard also gave me all the access to instructors I needed via e-mail, instant messaging, and real-time chats."

Online courses freed up enough time for Kim that she was able to accept a full-time job offer as a financial aid advisor at Ivy Tech–Richmond. Keeping the job was contingent on her completing her associate's degree, and online courses made it possible for her to finish her degree over the following year, despite the fact that she was soon diagnosed with stage IV, grade 3 cervical cancer. For three months Kim was getting radiation every day and chemotherapy on Friday. For two months during this period, she also got a surgical radiation treatment in a nine-hour procedure every Tuesday.

Meanwhile, she still worked 20 hours a week and, thanks to online courses, kept up her studies. Kim told me, "I decided not to take a leave of absence from school, because I was so close to finishing. I thought I could do course work while I was getting chemo. I did well in one online course that way, but I had to withdraw from a science course because I fell too far behind. Still, taking courses online allowed me to keep progressing."

The treatment was successful, and with her cancer in remission Kim got her associate's degree in July of 2008, only two months past the part-time school schedule she mapped out when she started in 2004. She graduated *cum laude* and a member of Phi

Theta Kappa, the community college counterpart to Phi Beta Kappa. In addition, she was a member of the All-Indiana Academic Team in Phi Theta Kappa's All-USA Community College Team competition, and was listed in *Who's Who in Junior Colleges.*

I'd be remiss if I didn't mention that in the final year of her studies for her associate's degree, while undergoing the intensive cancer treatment I described above, Kim also began serving as a veterans' representative at Ivy Tech–Richmond. She added that role to her job as a financial aid advisor in response to a call I issued for veterans' advisors and veterans' student groups on every Ivy Tech campus.

The veterans' student group Kim established has been extremely effective under her leadership. She recently wrote and submitted a successful $100,000 grant proposal to the Military Family Research Institute (MFRI). In awarding the grant to Ivy Tech–Richmond, MFRI noted that it had one of the most active veterans' groups in Indiana. At the second Indiana Statewide Student Veterans Organization Conference, held at Ivy Tech–Richmond in the spring of 2012, representatives from four-year schools—Ball State University, Indiana State University, Purdue University, Indiana University, and St. Mary of the Woods—were all eager to learn from Kim how to establish and sustain a good veterans' student group.

And Kim hasn't stopped pursuing her own higher education goals. She has transferred her associate's degree credits into an online bachelor's degree program in business administration at Franklin University of Ohio, and she is on track to graduate in May 2013.

Kim Wheeler Butts is obviously an extraordinary person, but her story illustrates the value that online courses provide to a wide variety of students.

■ ■ ■

How big a role online learning plays in your own higher education will depend on your personal needs, characteristics, and learning style, as well as your chosen course of study. Fields that require extensive practical or clinical training will likely always have on-campus and in-the-field components. Becoming a nurse, for example, requires that students spend a good deal of time learning-by-doing in a hospital. But indications are that online learning will eventually become valuable components of education and training in almost every field.

Community colleges across the country will continue to be at the forefront of these developments. We're making great strides in preparing students for online learning, developing new online courses and programs, and making access to student services and campus resources—admissions, financial aid, advising, library access, and so forth—available online. It's yet another example of why community college is such a smart choice for almost every student.

■ ■ ■

We've seen how community college can be a difference maker in your life. Now let's look at what you need to do be ready for college-level work.

Getting Ready for Community College

8

What You Should Do to Prepare for College-Level Work if You Are Now in High School

Enrolling at a community college is generally easy. The majority of schools have open admission policies, meaning that any and all students are welcome. In most states, all you need is a high school diploma or equivalent; high school students can enroll part-time. Grades aren't a factor, and SAT or ACT test scores aren't required. (However, you should keep in mind that some specialized community college programs, such as nursing and computer technology, have specific admission prerequisites and require separate applications. Furthermore, capacity constraints in California are now keeping some prospective students out of community college.)

The tests come after you enroll at community college. That's when you will almost certainly have to take a multiple-choice placement test to measure specific academic skills in reading, writing, math, and possibly other subjects. You also may have to write an essay. Two of the most common placement tests are the College Board's ACCUPLACER® and American College Testing's COMPASS test. These tests are designed to determine whether students need to take any remedial courses to help them prepare for the demands and complexity of college-level work. (For more on remediation, see Chapter 10, "The Placement Tests That Determine Where You Start in College.")

If your community college assigns you to remedial courses, you won't be alone. According to the Community College Research Center at Columbia University's Teachers College, about 60 percent of incoming community college students take at least one remedial course. Just like other courses, remedial classes cost money. However, the credits you earn usually do not count toward completing your certificate or degree program, which makes college longer and more expensive, including using up your financial aid.

My colleagues and I have seen many students succeed after taking remedial courses. Remediation offers students who may have struggled in high school a second chance for success. However, it's certainly preferable if you can get straight to work on your certificate or degree program. Research shows that only 25 percent of students in remedial classes go on to earn a community college credential or transfer to a four-year college. So your best bet is to prepare yourself for the higher-level work required in college before you get there, and to avoid remedial courses altogether.

The challenge of preparing yourself for college-level work and avoiding remedial classes will be different depending on your current situation. This chapter will look at what you should be doing if you are in high school now and will be going directly to community college. The next chapter will look at what you should be doing if you are in the workforce and will be going to community college as a career changer. But there is material in both chapters that is relevant no matter which category you are in, so you may well find it useful to read both.

Success Breeds Success

For most students, academic success in college begins with academic success in high school. Indeed, just because there are few academic obstacles to getting into a community college doesn't mean there is no connection between high school achievement and college success. It's therefore best to develop the prerequisite skills needed to succeed in college while you're still in high school.

Unfortunately, many community college students find themselves unprepared for the rigors of college course work. A 2010 study of California community college students by San Francisco–based independent research organization WestEd found that a significant number of interviewees said they experienced low expectations in high school and were not encouraged to take difficult courses of study. Because they knew they could attend a community college, they didn't think they needed to do more than merely pass their courses. Consequently, they found themselves unprepared for college-level work. These students wished in hindsight that they had applied themselves more, taken more challenging courses, and learned more about what to expect in college.

According to one student, "It's like, oh my gosh, I just basically wasted four years [in high school] by taking the easy track, when I should have taken the more advanced [track]." Another said, "I didn't have anyone during my high school years pushing me, [saying], 'You need all this because when you get to college, if you don't know it, you're going to start from rock bottom.'"

Many students in the 2010 California survey also said they hadn't learned much about community colleges while in high school and hadn't received information about what kinds of academic challenges to expect if they enrolled at a community college. Some said they might have changed their high school course sequence to prepare better if they had gotten more information.

The report also found that the majority of students knew little about placement tests before they enrolled at community college. Some weren't even aware such tests existed, whereas others didn't understand the stakes involved. Some students also didn't realize they could study for placement tests. One student said, "I thought it was one of those tests that you take just to see what kind of field they were going to recommend. And then I found out it places you in classes." Another said, "[The woman at the test center] said, 'It doesn't matter how you place. It's just to see where you are.' Looking back, that's not true. [How you place is] really important."

Another survey, conducted by Hart Research Associates for the College Board, looked at members of the high school graduating class of 2010. No matter what the students did after graduation— 43 percent enrolled in a four-year college, 25 percent in a two-year college, and 6 percent in a trade school, whereas 26 percent did not enroll in a postsecondary school—nearly half (47 percent) of all respondents said they wished they had worked harder in high school. And 44 percent said they wished they had taken different courses in high school as well. Of those, 40 percent wished they had taken more math courses; 37 percent wished they had taken more classes that prepared them for a specific job; and 33 percent wished they had taken more science courses.

With all of this in mind, ask yourself: How can—and should— you prepare for community college if you're still in high school? You must first recognize that community college is not merely an extension of high school. Community college is *college*. Whether it's a two- or four-year school, expectations are high. Indeed, as I've already mentioned in previous chapters, researchers have found no difference in the quality of instruction between community colleges and four-year institutions.

David Conley, chief executive officer of the Educational Policy Improvement Center, wrote the following in a report on college readiness for the Bill and Melinda Gates Foundation: "Students fresh out of high school may think a college course is very much like a similarly named high school class taken previously only to find out that expectations are fundamentally different. The college instructor is more likely to emphasize a series of key thinking skills that students, for the most part, do not develop extensively in high school."

To have a successful community college experience, you need to build on what you learn in high school. This begins with making informed decisions about which courses will best prepare you for college-level work in different fields. High school is the time to give some serious thought to fields you might want to major in when you get to college, and to discuss these ideas with parents, teachers, counselors, and other mentors.

However, this doesn't mean you have to set your college major and career decisions in stone in high school. You should always be open to exploring new areas as you advance in your education and your life. And you shouldn't shy away from science courses because you are mainly interested in the humanities, or vice versa. But as I told my own children when they were in high school, you *can* start to identify subject and career areas that you find most interesting and that are best suited to your talents. And this can help you begin to chart a path to develop your own unique abilities and interests in those areas.

In this regard, what you study in high school and how hard you study are both critically important. You not only need to have the necessary academic background to succeed; you must also know how to be organized and manage your time wisely. Advancing academically is like improving in a sport or getting better at playing a musical instrument. You've got to practice to improve, and high school is the time to hone the habits you need to succeed in college.

A Rigorous High School Curriculum Is the Best Preparation for College

In the words of one community college admissions director, "The best advice I can provide for students who plan on attending a community college is to take the same college-preparation courses in high school that they would take in preparation to attend any college." This sentiment is echoed by many education organizations, including the Pathways to College Network, which advises that all students—regardless of race/ethnicity, gender, disability, or socioeconomic status—should complete "an academically rigorous high school curriculum to be well-equipped for productive work and civic life."

An academically rigorous curriculum will emphasize analytical thinking, learning, comprehension, and writing skills. Demanding courses encompass both content and the development of cognitive abilities and key learning skills. Keep in mind that while such courses can be challenging, colleges look favorably on students who tackle them—even if they don't end up with As. These students fare better compared to students who take an easier track. (But don't sign up for higher-level courses before you satisfactorily complete lower-level ones.)

The College Board recommends that high school students take at least five "solid" academic classes every semester—that students "start with the basics and then move on to advanced courses." More specifically, the board recommends the subjects and classes detailed below "for success in high school and beyond, whether you plan to attend a four-year or two-year college."

English (Language Arts)

The message here is clear cut. Take English every year. Courses such as American and English literature will help you improve your writing skills, reading comprehension, and vocabulary.

The American Diploma Project (ADP) has published specific benchmarks in terms of skills needed for success in postsecondary education and beyond for English in eight categories: language, communication, writing, research, logic, informational text, media, and literature. For example, correct use of language is essential because "without fail, employers and college faculty cite correct grammar, usage, punctuation, capitalization and spelling as absolutely essential to success in classrooms and workplaces beyond high school."[1] Writing skills are equally important. It takes discipline to create, reshape, and polish a piece of writing. Learning to write well in high school will prepare you for occasions when you must write quickly and clearly on demand—whether in college classrooms or the workplace.

Math

Algebra and geometry have long been considered essential for success in college math classes and in many careers. If you take them early on, you'll be able to enroll in advanced science and math courses later in high school, and show colleges that you're ready for higher-level work. Most colleges look for students who have taken at least three years of math in high school, including courses like Algebra I, Algebra II, geometry, trigonometry, and calculus. According to the College Board, students who take Algebra I and geometry in high school have about an 80 percent chance of ending up in college, and students who successfully complete a math course higher than Algebra I double their chances of completing a bachelor's degree.

Why is math so important? The ADP puts it this way: "The study of mathematics is an exercise in reasoning." In addition to simply learning how to do math problems, students also need to learn more subjective skills, such as reading, interpreting, representing, and "mathematicizing" a problem. The report goes on to say, "As college students and employees, high school graduates will need to use mathematics in contexts quite different from the high school classroom. They will need to make judgments about what problem needs to be solved and, therefore, about which operations and procedures . . . [they should] apply."

Instead of listing specific courses, the ADP publishes high school mathematics benchmarks in four areas: number sense and numerical operations; algebra; geometry; and data interpretation, statistics, and probability.

Not every pathway in community college requires algebra. The trend in one-year professional certificates in areas such as machine tools, for example, is to embed applied math in job-specific practical instruction. I'll say more about this in Chapter 10. But although the kind of math in which you need to be proficient will vary depending on your goals, there is no doubt that math will be increasingly important for nearly all community college students.

Science

You also want to take at least three years of laboratory science classes in high school. A good combination includes two semesters each of biology, chemistry or physics, and Earth/space science. Some competitive schools may expect you to have taken four years of lab science courses.

A pamphlet from Harvard University's admissions office titled *Choosing Courses to Prepare for College* notes, "The natural sciences help to explain, to predict, and sometimes to control the processes responsible for phenomena that we observe. They constitute a large and growing portion of human knowledge important to everyone. Even if you have no intention of becoming a scientist, an engineer, or a physician, you should study some science throughout secondary school." Chemistry and physics in particular are "essential" subjects, as the pamphlet points out, because "the basic laws of chemistry and physics remain important and valid."[2]

Of course, you should be especially well-grounded in high school science and math if you plan to pursue a career in a STEM field—that is, science, technology, engineering, and mathematics. According to a recent survey by Microsoft, nearly four in five STEM college students said they decided to study STEM in high school or earlier. Yet only one in five STEM college students thought that their K–12 education prepared them extremely well for their college STEM courses. If you have ambitions to do something in STEM, the lesson is that you shouldn't take the minimum number of science and math courses your high school curriculum requires; you should take as many as you possibly can.

Social Studies

Studying the culture and history that have shaped the United States and the world will help you better understand local and world events taking place today. A good course plan includes U.S. history (two semesters), U.S. government (two semesters), world history or geography (one semester), plus one additional semester in a social studies course such as sociology, political science, comparative religious studies, or civics.

Foreign Languages

Students who study a foreign language show that they are willing to go beyond the basics. Although community colleges do not generally require foreign language study, students who intend to transfer to a four-year school should keep in mind that many bachelor's degree programs require at least two years of course work in the same foreign language and some prefer more. So you might as well begin preparing for that in high school. In an ever more connected world, with an increasingly global economy, knowing another language is more important and valuable than ever.

The Arts

Research shows that students who participate in the arts often do better in school and on standardized tests. According to the College Board, the arts "help you recognize patterns, discern differences and similarities, and exercise your mind in unique ways, often outside a traditional classroom setting." That is why it is a good idea to take at least one or two semesters in the arts, such as studio art, dance, music, or drama.

In addition, the College Board urges high school students to enroll in challenging classes such as AP® or honors courses. Research shows that students who score a 3 (out of 5) or higher on an AP exam typically experience greater academic success in college—and higher graduation rates—than students who do not take AP classes.

Completing an academically rigorous high school curriculum is the most important part of preparing to succeed in college. But it's not the only piece of the puzzle. What else can you do to prepare for college? The following are some other factors to consider:

- *Get to know your guidance counselor.* He or she will be a vital source of information on suggested courses, colleges, financial aid, scholarships, and more. However, high school guidance counselors have traditionally focused their higher-education recommendations on four-year colleges rather than community colleges. Although this is changing, you may need to take the initiative in asking your guidance counselor about the benefits of community college.
- *Participate in extracurricular activities*, such as school clubs, the student newspaper, sports, music, arts, and drama.
- *Work a summer job*, if possible. This experience teaches discipline, responsibility, teamwork, and other important skills that will be useful in college and beyond. Plus, it lets you earn money to supplement your college funds. If you can't find a paying job, look for an opportunity to volunteer.
- *Maintain an "achievement file"* with report cards, recommendations, awards, honors, school and community activities, and involvement in clubs.
- Take part in *weekend or summer enrichment programs*, workshops, or camps.
- *Read as much as possible* for fun and to learn about interesting subjects. The National Endowment for the Humanities has a recommended reading list for college bound students on its "Edsitement" website: http://edsitement.neh.gov/edsitements-reading-list-college-bound-students.

- *Get extra help for difficult classes* from tutors. If you receive a low grade in a class, consider repeating it during summer school if possible. Remember, colleges often view moderate success in harder courses more favorably than perfect grades in easier courses.
- *Talk to adults in various professions* about their careers and the education needed for each job.
- *Attend college fairs* and talk to different schools' representatives. *Visit colleges* and talk to current students.

Finally, in addition to content knowledge, preparing for college involves certain less tangible skills. Educator David Conley calls these habits of mind, academic behaviors, and contextual skills and awareness. He describes each of them as follows:

- *Habits of mind* are the "intelligent behaviors" necessary for college readiness, and they include intellectual openness, inquisitiveness, analysis, reasoning, argumentation, interpretation, precision, accuracy, and problem solving.
- *Academic behaviors* include self-monitoring ("the ability to think about how one is thinking") and study skills such as time management, preparing for and taking examinations, using information resources, taking class notes, and communicating with teachers and advisors.
- *Contextual skills and awareness* include amassing practical information, such as how to choose and apply to a college, receive financial aid, and adjust to college life. They also include developing an awareness and understanding of college culture, "and the human relations skills necessary to cope within this system even if it is very different from the community the student has just left." Many students who lack these particular skills become alienated, frustrated, and even humiliated during freshman year and decide to drop out, Conley asserts.

The college-ready student understands what is expected in a college course, can tackle the content knowledge that is presented, and can glean the key intellectual lessons the course was designed to convey.

■ ■ ■

Enrolling in a community college may turn out to be the best decision in your life. But to make the most of it, you have to prepare yourself before you enroll. Your chances of success will be much greater if you make the right decisions while in high school.

9

What You Should Do to Prepare for College-Level Work if You're Going to Community College as a Career Changer

If you need to make a career change, community college is very likely your best resource for doing so—and for making the change a successful one. As we saw in earlier chapters, earning a degree or a certificate at community college can build a bridge for you to walk across to a satisfying and rewarding new career.

If you're like most career changers, you'll have to go through community college while handling a lot more responsibility than the average student fresh out of high school. Most crucially, that will likely include responsibility to others in your family—children, spouse, partner, and/or elders—as well as responsibility to a job and other life issues.

That means you've really got to plan well and have lots of discipline and motivation. It means plenty of hard work. But if you dedicate yourself to the process and work through it step by step, you will have a great opportunity to recharge your life and achieve your American dream. That's happening in community college for tens of thousands of successful career changers.

Joining them begins with good preparation. That includes choosing a course of study and a community college and making sure you're ready for college, both academically in terms of your reading, writing, and math skills, and personally in terms of your whole life situation.

Plan to Succeed and Manage Time Well

In order to succeed in community college as a career changer, you've got to prepare yourself to do college-level work academically, and to handle the rest of your responsibilities alongside your studies. Preparing on both these fronts may take some time, which is one of the biggest areas of concern for career changers, who commonly believe that they have to make a change and get on with their lives as quickly as possible.

Time is precious and shouldn't be wasted. But you want to allow enough time to prepare well. If you rush, it will be harder for you to make good decisions about your new direction and the best way to progress in it. A sensible time frame for preparing for community college ideally begins four to six months before you enroll in your first-semester classes.

How much time you have to prepare and make decisions might be out of your control to some extent. If you're laid off unexpectedly, for example, or some other life-changing event occurs. In some states, programs that award retraining funds give recently dislocated workers only a few weeks to identify a community college degree or certificate program where they will use those funds. If you're in this sort of situation, you've got to work fast but smart, as you investigate possibilities and decide which one you will pursue. After that, you should still have some time to prepare to succeed in the course of study you've chosen.

As I'll have occasion to say more than once, career changers often run into trouble because they try to run before they can walk. A career change will affect every area of your life and will normally take a year or longer to accomplish. Don't be so impatient that you sabotage yourself. At every stage along the way it's a good idea to start with lots of small steps, build confidence and momentum as you progress, and then finish strong.

Don't Procrastinate

Make and take the time to prepare well for community college. But don't procrastinate. That's not really a contradiction. Use whatever time you have wisely by starting as soon as possible. Visit nearby community college campuses, explore community college websites, research interesting occupations on the Internet. And if you're not Internet savvy, put gaining computer and Internet skills high on your list of priorities; you'll find those skills are absolutely essential for today's community college students. From the start, look for helpful resources and services, which may be state or community based or in the community colleges themselves. This way you can begin to build the support network that you need to be a successful community college student.

A complicating factor here is that career changers commonly go through a mourning period. Losing a job can be as traumatic as losing a loved one. The feeling that one is trapped in the wrong job and anxiety about the future can also trigger mourning over a sense of lost opportunity. Such feelings can't just be dismissed, but you have to recognize that they're a normal stage that people making a career change go through. And then you have to move on and prepare to identify and realize new possibilities.

Find Your Field and Begin Building Your Support Network

Your first big decision is setting a new career goal. Depending on your situation and the economy in your region, or the region where you want to move, your goal may be to secure a better job in your current industry or to switch to a new industry. As you choose a direction for yourself, beware of being influenced too much by a "Top 50 Jobs" list. *Forbes* magazine puts out such a list, as do the federal and state governments. The problem with these lists is that they reflect hiring conditions at one point in time and will likely look different in several months. If you're not within six months of being able to apply for one of these jobs, you should ignore these lists and focus on identifying an occupation in which you can be successful.

Another common mistake in this regard is picking a future occupation based solely on the income it generally earns. Career changers often set their sights on nursing, for example, because it's a high-demand field that pays well and offers excellent stability. But not everyone will be happy or successful as a nurse. You have to find what's best for you, including your existing skills, interests, and abilities as well as those you will develop in community college.

In this regard, recognize and accept that a career change may well mean a step or two back in salary and level of responsibility, at least at first. You're more likely to make up lost ground, however, if you don't rush into things. Taking the time to make good decisions at the start of the process will help you go faster and further in the end.

To begin setting your new career goal, take a look at your life experience and accomplishments to date. You may have a better foundation to build on than you realize. In any case, you need to reach an honest assessment of your existing strengths and interests before you can pick a good next career goal.

Community, municipal, or state career services can be enormously helpful at this stage. If you are already going through the admissions process at a community college, the college's career services office should be a frequent destination for you. If you are working for a big employer and want to prepare yourself for a better job in the same company, there may be employer-provided career planning and career advancement resources you can use.

Use the Internet to find out if there is a U.S. Department of Education–funded Educational Opportunity Center (EOC) in your area. EOCs are designed to provide adult college students with a range of services, including career advising. Another important federally funded program for career changers is Veterans Upward Bound. Both programs are part of an initiative called TRIO, so named because it originally included three postsecondary student support programs (there are now eight related programs in TRIO: http://www2.ed.gov/about/offices/list/ope/trio/index.html).

Seeking out career services help early, well before you start your first-semester classes, should set a pattern for you of seeking appropriate help and support at every stage of your journey as a community college student. Career changers often think that they should be able to handle problems, big or small, on their own. They're often embarrassed and ashamed to ask for help. That's counterproductive. Sometimes you need assistance precisely to keep a small problem from mushrooming into a big one.

Being a successful community college student demands self-reliance and individual motivation, discipline, and hard work. But that doesn't mean you should never get assistance with a problem. When you are in community college, you will need to tap a variety of resources and services appropriately in and out of the classroom. You will benefit from doing the same thing as you prepare to enter community college and do college-level course work.

The people involved in providing those resources and services, from career planning to financial aid to academic advising, will be happy to see you. They know that the more a student is plugged into all the available resources and services, the more likely that student is to succeed. This is true from the start of the process: Statistics show that students who get career planning help early on are far more likely to complete their degree or certificate programs and achieve their career goals.

After helping you to assess your current strengths accurately, a career services advisor can also help you to plot a new career path. Although you shouldn't fixate on the "Top 50 Jobs" of the moment, you should look carefully at long-term job growth trends in your region or, if you are contemplating a move, the region where you would like to live. Then you can map your strengths and interests against occupations where demand for workers is growing. For some good ideas about which occupations to target, see Chapter 4.

When you identify some good potential occupations, consider whether there is someone you know or can identify in your community who works in one of those areas. Try to talk to that person about what the job is like. Perhaps you can do some job shadowing, as it is known, tagging along with the person at his or her job for a day or two. This can be a good way to test whether a job is really right for you, although you should keep in mind that one person's experience of a job may be very different from another's.

In any case, after you have picked a new career path, you have to ask what you need to become a desirable job candidate in that area. Work backward from the job goal to the course of study that will prepare you for it. If you don't yet have a higher education credential, what associate's degree or professional certificate will position you to get the job you want? If you already have an associate's degree, should you return to community college with an eye to transferring up to a four-year degree program? Or maybe you already have a bachelor's or even a master's degree, but the degrees are in low-demand areas. In that case, will it benefit you most if you take that master's degree off your résumé and concentrate on building a new set of credentials with an associate's degree or a certificate in a high-demand area?

After you've identified your career goal and the course of study it requires, it's time to find a community college where you feel comfortable and welcome and where you can do that course of study. Go beyond looking online at the school's website to see that they have such-and-such a program. Go on campus to meet the program chair and talk to him or her about how the program is designed, the time and courses required to complete it, and your own goals and academic background. You may feel shy about discussing these things, but doing so will help the program chair advise you on whether a program is right for you and what you need to do to prepare for it. (See Chapter 12, "If You're Going to Community

College as a Career Changer," if you've entered or are entering community college without having set a definite career goal.)

During this period of research into the right career path for you, begin devoting time regularly to searching the Internet for scholarships. Many small and not-so-small scholarships go unused. Search under "adult community college scholarship" combined in various ways with your intended course of study, your region of the country, and other factors that might describe your particular situation, such as minority background or being a first-generation college student. I recently heard about a career changer at Ivy Tech who paid for her entire nursing program with scholarships she found on the Internet. There are many other similar examples. The time you spend looking for scholarships online can be tedious, but it has a big potential payback. You may also be eligible for federally funded student financial aid as either a full-time or part-time student; see Chapter 3, "Scholarships and Financial Aid."

Once you've settled on your new career path and the community college you will attend (you should keep looking for scholarships online), lay out a written plan for achieving your goal. As your preparation continues, and you learn more about what your course of study requires, you should revise the plan and make it more detailed. After you start community college, you should continue to keep this plan current and chart your progress against it.

Pat Cumber, who describes herself as "an older student," was laid off as a machinist and decided to change careers and pursue her passion for food. The married mother of five enrolled at Fox Valley Tech in Appleton, Wisconsin, and earned an associate's degree in marketing in 2011. She also earned a certificate in entrepreneurship, which helped her launch her business Food Tailor, a food truck that serves international cuisine with a home-style flair. "My education at Fox Valley taught me how to get my name out there, create a business plan, and launch my business," she says.

She is currently studying for a second associate's degree in culinary arts so that she can create new dishes for Food Tailor. She works 30 to 40 hours a week on the food truck with her husband,

and they support their family on its profits. "My biggest challenge was believing in myself that I could have my own business. I was a machinist for many years and didn't know anything about marketing or setting up a business. Fox Valley Tech gave me the tools to follow my dream," she says.

Academic Preparation

As I've said before, community college is college. If you don't have any experience of higher education, you need to know that the course work will be much more demanding than the usual high school curriculum. If you haven't been in school for 10, 20, or more years, you also need to keep in mind that there is a new world of education, which runs by e-mail and electronic course management systems like Blackboard (see Chapter 7, "On Campus or Online?"). If you are not computer and Internet savvy, in the sense of being comfortable navigating the web and having good basic keyboarding skills, gaining these skills and becoming familiar with the technology and terminology should be high on your to-do list.

Your community college probably offers a course in these computer skills and related study skills. But if you can gain the basic computer skills you need before you start your first semester at community college, so much the better. You might want to do this informally on your own or with the help of a tech-savvy friend or relative, but a computer skills course in an adult education program will almost certainly get you up to speed faster.

The change from pencils, pens, and typewriters to computers hasn't lessened the importance of reading, writing, and math skills. In a technology-based knowledge economy and job market, they're more important than ever. If you haven't been in school for a long time and you haven't been doing much reading, writing, or math on the job, your skills in these areas are probably rusty.

One of the best and most important things you can do to prepare for college-level reading and writing is to start reading more.

In general, more reading is valuable, no matter what the subject matter. But you should make an effort to read more serious books, especially nonfiction books on topics related to your course of study. You should also go online or to the library and look for specialized journals in the field you're going to study. Getting used to reading more formal texts will help you a lot with your course work.

Write practice reports on what you read, and ask any family members and friends who can do so to give you feedback on them. Go to an online writing lab for more structured writing exercises and feedback, or to a writing lab or workshop in a community-based adult education program.

You can find lots of math instruction and brush-up help for free online. Khan Academy (www.khanacademy.org) and Purplemath (www.purplemath.com) both have good resources in these areas. For example, Khan Academy has examples of how to work through the math problems on the California High School Exit Examination (CAHSEE). If you can handle the math section of the CAHSEE, you should be ready for college-level math.

Your community college's website probably will have material related to its placement test, including a sample test with reading, writing, and math sections. You should familiarize yourself well with this test before you take it, especially if you have not taken a standardized test for many years (see Chapter 10, "The Placement Tests That Determine Where You Start in College").

Taking the practice placement test will give you a sense of your current skill levels. If your reading, writing, and/or math skills need more than brushing up, look for a free adult education course in your community (EOCs offer them, as do most public school systems) or at your community college.

Treat working on your reading, writing, and math skills as practice for when you have course work to do. Begin to establish a routine in which you have set times for studying and working on assignments.

In this regard, you need to understand the enormous time investment that college courses require. A good rule of thumb is

10 hours a week per course, including both class time and doing required reading and assignments. In summer sessions, you should allow 15 hours a week per course. The hours per week should go up in summer because summer sessions are accelerated; they condense the usual 16-week semester's course content into 8 to 10 weeks with longer class times and more homework.

With that in mind, let's look at the importance of preparing for college's impact on the rest of your life.

Getting Your Life Ready for College

Getting ready for college academically is only part of the preparation you should be doing. Going to college will affect every aspect of your life.

Are you going to have to work full time or part time while you go to college? Will you be working during the day, or at nights and on weekends? If it's possible financially, you should consider working less when you start college. You have to balance the immediate income against how college will pay off in the long run.

If you have a family, everyone in the family will need time to adjust to your being in college. They will surely want to support you and help you succeed, but they might not know the best way to do so, especially if they have not been to college themselves. The same goes for relationships with significant others and friends.

It can be especially hard for children to understand why a parent has to devote so much time to school and sometimes can't be available to them. One good way to have a conversation with the family about the new demands on your time is to write out your practice study schedule and put it on the refrigerator. Let everyone know that you need to devote that time to study, explain why it will help you and the family, and ask for their understanding and help. If you have children who are in school, doing some of your studying while they are doing theirs can help them feel a part of what you are doing.

The period before you start your first-semester courses is also the time when you should identify and start using a personal support system that includes family members, friends, and others, such as a minister or other trusted mentors and advisors. Keep them posted on your progress in preparing for college, and consult with them regularly to help keep yourself on track to achieving your goals.

As you approach your first semester, take an honest look at your life and recalculate how much time you are going to have for college. One of the most common ways career changers stumble is by overloading themselves in their first semester. Don't expect yourself to be superhuman and hold down a full-time job while going to school full time and still have time and energy for your family or personal life. Be realistic. Again, the formula for success in college, as in most things in life, is to take lots of small steps at first, build your confidence as you go, and then finish strong. For more on balancing college and the rest of your life, see Chapter 12, "If You're Going to Community College as a Career Changer."

■ ■ ■

Now let's take a look at the placement tests most community colleges will use to determine where you start in college.

10 The Placement Tests That Determine Where You Start in College

Imagine yourself ready to start your first community college courses. Maybe you're entering college directly after graduating from high school, or maybe you're returning to school after some time in the workforce. Either way, you're excited to be in college. Although you're a little nervous about the challenges ahead, you feel eager and ready to meet them.

However, the community college doesn't agree that you are ready for college-level work. It's given you a placement test in reading, writing, and math, and your scores in these areas mean you have to take remedial courses (also called developmental education courses) in one or more of these subjects. It feels like you've been thrown back into high school. You're disappointed, bewildered, demoralized, even ashamed. You could even begin to think that maybe college isn't for you.

Don't think that way. For one thing, you're not alone, and large numbers of community college students are placed in remedial courses. There are many reasons that can contribute to students' being unprepared for college-level work. Career changers may not have been able to free up time from work and family responsibilities to improve or refresh their reading, writing, and math skills. Some high school students simply don't take preparing for college seriously enough. Others have tried their best, but have been hampered by circumstances outside their control. This is often the case for students from low-income backgrounds who are the first generation in their family to enter college. Students are at a real disadvantage without parents who have been there and done that, and who can explain what will be expected of them in college.

Kindergarten to twelfth-grade (K–12) educational policies and grade inflation also have a lot to do with students' not being ready for college. Too many states have watered down the standards for promotion from one year of school to another and for graduation from elementary, middle, and high school. They have traded academic rigor for graduation rates, and have focused more on moving students through the system than on preparing them to succeed at the next level.

The situation in New York City is typical of what's happening across the country. From 2005 to 2010 the public high school graduation rate in New York City rose from 46.5 percent to 61 percent. This means a lot more New York City public high school students passed the New York State Board of Regents exams for high school graduation. What also rose, however, was the number of New York City community college students who needed remedial developmental education in reading, writing, and math. In 2005 the percentage of students in remedial classes in all three subjects was 15.4 percent, whereas in 2010 it was 22.6 percent. "Over all," the *New York Times* reported in the fall of 2011, "74 percent of city high school graduates enrolled at the [City University of New York's] six community colleges take remediation in at least one subject."[1]

A follow-up story in the *New York Times* revealed that "the college readiness rate [for New York City high school students in 2011] was less than half the graduation rate." In some cases the disparity was even more extreme. One New York City public high school had a four-year graduation rate of over 90 percent, but a college readiness rate of only around 15 percent. At another public high school, 100 percent of the students graduated in four years, but fewer than 25 percent of them were ready for college-level work.[2]

This is not to pick on New York City. According to Complete College America, over 50 percent of the nation's community college students take a remedial course in reading, writing, or math. Obviously, K−12 education is where this problem ultimately has to be solved, so that the majority of students graduate high school ready for postsecondary education. In the meantime, significant numbers of community college students will have to grapple with developmental education challenges. It is the first real "go/no go" gateway that many students have ever faced in their educational experience.

A good many students also struggle in four-year schools because they are not truly ready for college-level work. But the numbers are higher in community colleges, thanks to the fact that our student bodies are much more diverse in terms of educational and income backgrounds. As I've noted in earlier chapters, community college enrollments represent the entire spectrum of students, from those who are well-prepared academically to those who are not.

In the last two chapters we looked at strategies and tactics for getting ready for college-level work, depending on whether you are entering community college directly from high school or after some time in the workforce or raising a family. As I emphasized in those chapters, if you approach preparing for college in a serious, dedicated way, you're very likely to make a successful transition into community college. You'll have to work hard to fulfill your potential and make the most of the experience, but you'll have the foundation in academic knowledge and study skills to take demanding college courses in stride.

In this chapter I'll offer some additional tips on avoiding remedial courses. And I'll tell you about promising new trends in community colleges' handling of remedial education. These trends are making remedial education much more student friendly than has traditionally been the case, and they are proving to be effective in accelerating college progress and increasing degree and certificate completion for those students who need remediation.

Naturally, you will want to avoid remedial courses if at all possible. Depending on how your school and state structure their remedial programs, and on whether you have to take remedial courses more than once to pass them, being placed in remedial courses can delay your start in college-level courses for three semesters or more. In California, it can even delay enrolling in community college to begin with. Because there are far too few seats in its community colleges for all the students seeking them, California no longer lets students enroll if their placement test scores are too low.

No matter where you're going to community college, being placed in remedial courses can wind up costing you a significant amount of money and time. Even if most or all of your major expenses are covered by financial aid, you still are likely to have added incidental and/or living expenses that you will need to cover out of your own pocket—and, of course, the longer it will be before you can complete your degree or certificate and start achieving other academic, career, and life goals.

Remedial courses can also have a significant impact on your financial aid. Federally funded student financial aid will pay for a maximum of 30 credit hours of remedial courses. If students have to take remedial courses in all three subject areas, they may have to progress through three levels of pre-college math and two levels each of reading and writing. That typically means seven courses of three or more credit hours each, which can easily push students over the 30-credit-hour limit. At that point they will have to pay for their remedial courses out of pocket.

It's no wonder that statistics show that the more time students have to spend in remedial courses, the less likely they are to complete a degree or certificate program. There are just too many exit points along the way where students give up in frustration.

It doesn't have to turn out that way, however. Remediation can be effective if you approach it with the right attitude and discipline. In this regard there is one thing I urge you to take to heart. Needing remedial courses does not mean you lack the smarts for college. It only means you are not yet prepared enough for college-level work. With good planning and hard work, you can succeed in remedial courses and go on to succeed in a degree or certificate program.

Now let's look at the details of how community colleges assess students' college readiness, and what you can do to be college ready as soon as possible.

The Placement Process

Before you register for any courses, the overwhelming majority of community colleges will give you a standardized placement test with reading, writing, and math components. Most community colleges use one of two tests: the COMPASS test offered by American College Testing or the ACCUPLACER test offered by the College Board. Both tests have multiple-choice sections for math, reading, and writing (the questions for writing mainly involve sentence structure, grammar, and spelling). The COMPASS test has an optional essay-writing section.

Ivy Tech has adopted the ACCUPLACER test, and the "Additional Resources" Appendix in this book includes a sample test you can take. If the college you are going to uses the COMPASS test, you should still find it very useful because of the overall similarity in the tests' structure and content.

Some community colleges and community college systems have their own assessment tests. For example, as part of the City University of New York (CUNY), New York City's six community colleges use CUNY's own multiple-choice assessment tests. The National Center for Public Policy and Education reported in 2007 that "nearly 100 different examinations are used for placement purposes" at California community colleges. But again, all the various assessment tests have the same general structure and content. So if you're a prospective student at one of these colleges, the sample test in the Appendix should still be useful to you.

Not all community colleges administer placement tests. Some schools make placement decisions based on other criteria, including your high school record and other standardized tests you may have taken, such as the ACT, SAT, and PSAT/NMSQT®.

The first step to avoiding remedial courses, or progressing through them successfully, is to ask lots of questions. To begin with, ask yourself, "Am I ready for college-level work?" For help in answering this question, see Chapter 8, "What You Should Do to Prepare for College-Level Work if You Are Now in High School," or Chapter 9, "What You Should Do to Prepare for College-Level Work if You're Going to Community College as a Career Changer."

If you are in high school now, and you have even one more semester ahead of you, consider adjusting your course load to include a math course, even if you've already fulfilled your math requirements. As I explained in Chapter 8, many states have high school math requirements that will not adequately prepare you for college-level work. A minimal math requirement can be even more counterproductive for college-bound students if a school system uses block course scheduling. A typical progression in many public school systems is for students to take Algebra I in the eighth grade, geometry in the ninth grade, and Algebra II in the tenth grade. If block scheduling means you complete Algebra II in the fall of your sophomore year, you will have two and a half academic years without any math before you get to college. That's too long a break to keep your math skills in decent shape.

Likewise, if you still have at least one more semester ahead of you, make sure you take a class that requires writing research papers. The ability to write a research paper is essential for success in college-level courses.

Ideally, as I said in Chapter 8, you should take English and social studies courses that require writing research papers, and math courses (or science courses with a math component) throughout high school. Being a student is like being an athlete. Every serious athlete has a rigorous off-season conditioning program. You have to keep your academic muscles and skills in good condition, too, even if your high school's requirements give you the freedom to take it easy as you approach graduation. Taking it easy in the short term can make your life a lot harder in the long term.

If you are returning to school as a career changer, look for a basic adult education skills course or refresher course. In most states these are offered free of charge through the state department of education or the workforce development arm of the state department of labor. If you work for a large employer, you also may be able to get educational services or assistance through your job. If you have older children in high school or college, recruit them to help you study and review reading, writing, and math. My colleagues at Ivy Tech and I have seen more than one older student benefit from this strategy.

During the application and enrollment process, you should also ask questions of the community college(s) you are considering. Most community colleges have information on their websites about the assessment test they use and preparation for it. The resources a school provides may include sample questions, review sessions, and study guides.

Depending on what you can find on your prospective community college's website, you may also need to ask some or all of the following questions:

- Does the school administer a placement test?
- Is there a fee for the test?
- Does the school use COMPASS or ACCUPLACER?
- Does the school have test prep resources and services for entering students?
- Can ACT, SAT, or PSAT scores be substituted for taking the placement test? Many community colleges across the country

have rules for substituting ACT, SAT, or PSAT scores for the COMPASS or ACCUPLACER test.

- If the assessment test score places a student into remedial courses, can the student take the test again to try to raise the score?
- Is there a fee for a retest?
- Is there a limit to how many times a student can take the assessment test?

As I'll discuss more in Part IV, "How to Succeed in Community College," one of the keys to success as a college student is learning to be an effective advocate for yourself. Students entering college directly from high school might be used to having their parents ask questions and advocate for them. That's not appropriate in college. For their part, older students who are returning to school after being in the workforce or raising their families might be used to advocating for themselves in their daily lives, but be hesitant about doing so in a community college setting that is unfamiliar and at times bewildering.

Whether you are entering college directly from high school or after a period of time out of school, you must be able to assert yourself effectively. Never hesitate to ask a question that concerns you, but always conduct yourself politely. Remember that community college faculty and staff are on your side and want to help you. Don't make that difficult for them by being abrasive or confrontational.

Preparing for the Test

Once you have determined how your community college handles its placement test—assuming you don't place out of it by meeting the school's individual criteria for doing so—you've got to prepare for it. Take the test seriously. Don't be cavalier and "Christmas tree" it, as students sometimes say, meaning they filled in answers at random. For all the reasons I've noted above, taking the assessment test casually can really cost you.

You should avail yourself of all the test prep resources your prospective community college offers. Savvy students also use the Internet to search for test prep and review materials. There is a lot of good stuff out there that is completely free of charge (see the "Additional Resources" Appendix for some examples).

The websites for the COMPASS (www.act.org/compass) and ACCUPLACER (www.collegeboard.com/student/testing/accuplacer) tests also have free test prep material. ACCUPLACER sells a $1.99 app for the iPhone, iPod Touch, and iPad that includes interactive practice tests for arithmetic, elementary algebra, college-level math, reading comprehension, and sentence skills.

Last, there are test prep and review books available for both the COMPASS and ACCUPLACER tests.

You can usually take your community college's placement test as soon as you've been accepted to enroll there. You should give yourself time to prepare for the test. But don't wait too long, either. If you don't take the test until just before the semester starts, you may not have time to do a retest with an adequate review period first.

Standardized Test-Taking Techniques

Reviewing for the test is one thing. Actually taking the test is another. If you're entering community college directly from high school, you undoubtedly have lots of experience with standardized tests. If you're entering community college as a career changer, you may not be so familiar with them. In either case, here are a few tips that have worked for standardized test takers over the years:

- Familiarize yourself with the test well ahead of taking it.
- Get a good night's sleep and eat properly before the test.
- Be aware of time and pace yourself. Every few questions, take a deep breath and relax your muscles.

- Read the question and all the multiple choice answers completely and thoroughly before you choose an answer.
- Where there is a reading comprehension passage followed by questions, *read the questions first*. This primes your brain to spot the answers as you read the passage.
- If you don't know the answer to a true/false question, guess "true," which is statistically more likely because of how the questions tend to be written.
- Crossing out the obviously wrong answers in a multiple choice question makes it easier to concentrate on the remaining choices. If you can eliminate two wrong answers, your chances of picking the right answer go way up.
- Scan the question for key words and phrases to guide your choice of an answer.
- When doing math problems on scratch paper, take a moment to ensure you have written out the problem correctly before solving it.
- If you work out a math problem and your answer doesn't match any of the answer choices, reread the problem and start over.
- Remember that earlier questions tend to be easier than later questions.
- Don't guess blindly, but trust your first guess.

After the Test

Okay, you've taken the test, and to your dismay it places you into remedial courses. Before you resign yourself to registering for those courses, honestly ask yourself if you could do better with more review—assuming that the school will let you take the test again. Maybe you had a bad day for one reason or another. If you feel that the placement into remedial courses does not truly reflect your abilities, you owe it to yourself to do a retest—after a more intensive review to prepare yourself to do your best.

When all is said and done, you may still need to take remedial courses. Across the country, community colleges use three main models for these courses. Remedial practices often apply on a statewide basis, but it is possible that you will have a choice between community colleges that use different models.

The traditional model is for students to do all their remedial education courses on a block schedule during the regular semester before moving on to college-level courses. In California this can mean up to three semesters of nothing but remedial courses before students can begin their degree or certificate program courses. That assumes students don't have to repeat any remedial courses, in which case it could take even longer for them to progress to college-level courses.

As I said at the start of the chapter, this often demoralizes students and leads to lots of them dropping out of college. The success rate for students in block remediation programs, unfortunately, is below 10 percent. And even if students remain committed to school and eventually succeed academically, spending more than a semester in remedial classes can create financial aid problems, as I mentioned earlier.

Seeking a better way, community colleges are trying two alternative forms of remediation. One is to give students who need remediation in all three areas of reading, writing, and math a semester in which they work intensively on only these skills. Based on this model, CUNY's six community colleges have implemented a program called Start. A full-time version of Start puts students in the classroom for five hours a day, five days a week. A part-time version requires attendance for 12 hours a week during afternoons and evenings. What makes the Start program especially attractive is its extremely low cost of only $75, compared to normal full-time tuition at CUNY's community colleges of $1,800 a semester in 2011–2012. The early results are promising, although it will be a challenge to expand such a program to serve more students and keep the cost so low.

Another promising new model for remedial courses is just-in-time remediation, also known as concurrent or corequisite remediation. In this model, a student takes an entry-level college course in tandem with a supplemental remedial course that supports it. It is like having a full-time tutor. The idea is to give students the remedial help they need in stages, as they progress through their degree or certificate program work. The Community College of Baltimore County (CCBC) in Maryland is one of the schools that has pioneered this approach. For example, a student at CCBC who needs remediation in writing will enroll in an entry-level college composition course back to back with a remedial writing course.

At Ivy Tech we are moving to this corequisite, just-in-time model for our remedial courses in reading, writing, and math. As in the CCBC example, Ivy Tech students take a gateway entry-level college course in a subject area and pair that with a supplemental remedial course in the same area.

On the math side, we're also working with the Charles A. Dana Center of the University of Texas—Austin to structure math pathways for specific majors and professional certificates. In our welding, HVAC, and machine tools certificate programs, for example, we've embedded remedial math modules that contain the applied math that each stage of a program requires.

Ivy Tech students who need remediation have been enthusiastic supporters of the just-in-time approach, because it enables them to start work on their degree or certificate from day one. They no longer feel like they're being sent back to a high school classroom and treated like second-class students who aren't good enough for "real" courses. They say that pairing a college-level course with a remedial course that supports it helps them to consolidate their learning, and it shows in their grades. If our early results are typical, corequisite, just-in-time remediation will have a significant positive effect on degree and certificate completion for many students.

■ ■ ■

For the various reasons examined in this chapter, remedial courses are no student's first choice. But they can be a stepping-stone to success in community college—and the rest of your life—if you approach them with the right attitude and effort. Whether or not you need remedial courses, let me now offer you some thoughts and tips on how to make the most of your community college experience.

IV

How to Succeed in Community College

11 If You're Going to Community College Directly from High School as a Full-Time Student

Yo've heard the old saying, "Genius is one percent inspiration, 99 percent perspiration." Well, it just happens to be true. Being a full-time community college student requires time, dedication, and hard work—and not just in the classroom.

As a community college student, you will be asked to perform at a much higher level than you may be used to, and you also will be challenged in other ways. Embrace those challenges! They will help prepare you for whatever obstacles you may face later in life.

The transition from high school to college is difficult. You're expected to manage your own time and your own schedule. Much of the work is done outside of classes. There's very little hand holding. College students have much more freedom than high school students, but freedom comes with responsibilities.

Many new students struggle to succeed in the community college environment. They may have entered college thinking it was just an extension of high school, only to discover that classes are much more demanding, and expectations are higher. They may have thought that it was "only community college," not realizing that courses are just as demanding as those in four-year institutions (if they weren't, you wouldn't be able to transfer your credits after two years).

Some students end up lowering their academic goals, or, worse, dropping out altogether. According to a 2007 study of California community college students issued by Policy Analysis for California Education (PACE), a research center based at the University of California–Berkeley and Stanford University, the majority of young adults in two-year colleges enter with the goal of transferring to a four-year college to earn a bachelor's degree, but only a minority make it beyond the first semester with those goals intact. One possible explanation: The students did not fully appreciate the academic and other challenges they would face in college.

Community colleges are addressing these issues by offering what are variously known as "success," "academic skills," or "academic strategies" courses for new students. For instance, at Houston (Texas) Community College (HCC), all freshmen are required to enroll in a success course unless they have already completed 12 college credit hours. The course is designed to prepare HCC students for the demands of college and beyond, with lessons in setting priorities, time management, effective listening, note taking, information retention, book analysis, and test taking. According to the Center for Community College Student Engagement, students who take a success course are more likely to complete their other courses, earn better grades, have higher overall GPAs, and earn degrees. Tulsa (Oklahoma) Community College requires some incoming students to take an "academic strategies" course. Those students are 20 percent more likely to remain enrolled than students who do not take the course, and they perform better in their classes.

If your community college offers a success course, by all means take it. If not, consider these strategies for college success.

Courses. Choose them carefully. It's easy to get lost in the vast array of offerings and fill up on "empty calorie" credit hours. Don't lose sight of your program of study. And the sooner you decide on a program, the better. Research shows that the sooner community college students enter a concentration, the more likely they are to succeed. In one study, more than half of students who entered a program of study in their first year earned a community college credential or transferred to a four-year college within five years. By contrast, only about a third of students who entered a program of study in their second year completed a credential or transferred. Make sure that you are choosing courses that are transferable to colleges and universities.

Time management. Successful students are good at juggling multiple assignments and activities while setting aside time for nonschool activities, such as exercise, meals, and personal relationships. At the beginning of each quarter or semester, create a schedule and try to follow it carefully until it becomes a routine. Set priorities. If you feel overwhelmed, cut back on an activity or two. Allow more time for difficult classes. As a general rule, you should plan on spending 10 hours a week on every class, including class time, studying, and doing assignments. Break assignments into manageable segments. Don't wait until the last minute to do assignments, particularly major research projects. Build in extra time for unexpected events. One of the biggest differences between high school and college is that parents and teachers aren't around to tell you what to do. You're in charge of your own destiny.

Attendance. It goes without saying that you should attend classes, right? Yes, but many college students think that it's no big deal to skip an occasional class or more. It turns out that class attendance is a major predictor for college success, even more so than high school GPAs, SAT scores, and other standardized admissions tests. Unlike high school, where teachers take regular attendance at the beginning of every class, community college instructors often forgo the practice, especially in large lecture courses. That makes it tempting for some students to skip class and rely on notes or recordings from peers. Resist the temptation. You'll miss important information, and you'll deny yourself the opportunity to participate in class discussions and exercises. You'll also create more work for yourself, since you'll have to catch up on the lecture material later. Even in large lecture classes, professors notice who's there and who's not. Students who attend classes develop important relationships with their instructors, and they make connections with other students. Remember, you've made a conscious choice to attend community college. You have goals and ambitions. Don't blow your chances of achieving those goals and ambitions by skipping class.

Note taking. Taking notes in class—whether on paper or on a laptop or tablet computer—is critical for understanding course material and studying for tests. The very act of writing while listening to a lecture forces you to pay close attention. But effective note taking does not mean writing down every single word spoken by the instructor. Decide what's important and what isn't. Write in phrases, not in full sentences, using abbreviations (but make sure you can read your notes later). Use a separate notebook for each class. Sometimes your professor will tell you what you will need to know later; other times he or she will repeat information, summarize material, or write main points on the board. These are good cues for note taking. If your instructor gives specific real-life or hypothetical examples, write those down. Don't write something down if you don't understand it; ask the professor to explain it. Make sure your notes are legible and well-organized; you will need to review them later before tests. If possible, review your notes immediately after class; this helps with memory retention.

Test taking. Let's face it: Taking a test is never fun. Even the most successful college students usually experience some anxiety before a test. However, there are steps you can take to make the process less painful, and help you end up with a better grade. First and foremost, don't wait until the last minute to start studying. Begin reviewing material at least several days before the test, and break up the process by studying two or three hours a day. Leaving things to the night before the test is a recipe for poor performance. No matter how many hours you cram, you are going to be underprepared. And the physical toll of cramming and not getting enough sleep will also ensure that you cannot do your best.

So allow ample time to review the material the exam will cover. As part of your review, create a pretest with questions based on the study guide or notes from class. Give yourself a time limit and answer the questions without referring to your notes or textbook. Get plenty of sleep the night before the actual test, and arrive at class early on exam day. Read the test instructions carefully; the last thing you want to do is answer a different question from one that's on the test. Before you start answering questions or writing essays, review the entire test and determine how much time you should spend on each question. It's okay to answer the easy questions first, but allow enough time to go back to the more difficult questions. If you have some time left when you are finished, look over the test to make sure you have answered all of the questions. Make sure your full name is on the test.

Study habits. Successful college students know how to study effectively and efficiently. They have developed a study routine depending on their schedule, and they stick to it. Research shows that the most successful college students study at least 20 hours a week. At the beginning of each term, find a quiet place to study and create a schedule of the hours you'll be at work. (Some students prefer to alternate between several study locations.) If you have an hour or two between classes, use that time to review material and catch up on reading assignments. As you study, take notes and prepare a list of questions. (Writing notes helps you remember the material.) Use a highlighter, but avoid the temptation to highlight entire pages. Take breaks while studying to stay alert. Some students build rewards into their study schedule. For example, two hours of studying followed by a half hour of phone calls or texts to friends, then back to work. Remember, build in time during your day for relaxation. If you spend all of your time studying, you'll burn out fast.

Study groups. Research shows that students who work in groups develop an increased ability to solve problems and show a greater understanding of the material being taught. Many successful students swear by study groups. Studying with others can help keep you motivated, and you may learn information that you otherwise might have missed. You can discuss key points and get help on a confusing concept. Study groups can also be more efficient than studying alone; you can cover more ground if you divide tasks and share results. Because study groups meet at regular times, you cannot procrastinate. They provide a built-in support system for students, too. After all, members have the same goal of succeeding in the class.

Studying with others is more fun than studying alone, but keep in mind that if you're trying to study with your best friends, you may not get much studying done. Many college students (and professors) are now using social media sites, such as Facebook, to organize study groups, discuss course readings with classmates, or ask questions of professors. These online get-togethers and discussions can be as effective as meeting in person. But again, if you and your classmates are having a study jam with social media, make sure that it doesn't degenerate into socializing.

Writing. David Conley, director of the Center for Educational Policy Research, has said, "The ability to write well is the single academic skill most closely associated with college success." College students are expected to write clearly, cogently, and extensively across many disciplines. In most classes—even some science and technology classes—writing is how you will be evaluated, either on tests or research papers. Your writing shows how you think and what facts you know. The ability to make a coherent argument, rather than simply regurgitate facts, is central to much college writing. Successful students are able to convey their knowledge and their ideas effectively through writing. They write, rewrite, and revise again. They look up unfamiliar words. They know how to use a style manual. They avoid plagiarism by citing sources consistently. They start early on long-term papers, and they prepare outlines before they begin writing.

Many students struggle with writing. Community colleges have responded by offering remedial writing courses, which may be required of some students. Some colleges also have writing centers, with coaches who provide students with professional assistance. If your college has a writing center, take advantage of what it has to offer.

College resources. If you simply show up for classes at your community college and then leave, you'll be doing yourself a disservice. Successful students are engaged with their schools—with their advisors, with their professors, with their peers. Find out when your instructors have office hours and try to visit each of them at least once per term. If you need extra help, reach out to them. This applies to tutors, mental health counselors, financial aid officers, career counselors, and librarians; don't be afraid to take advantage of these important human resources. Seeking help is a sign of strength and resourcefulness, not of weakness. According to the 2009 Community College Survey of Student Engagement, students who have personal relationships with faculty members, college employees, and other students are more likely to succeed and reach their educational goals. If your school offers orientation services for new students, sign up for them. Research shows that participation in orientation leads to greater use of college support services and improved retention of at-risk students.

Health and well-being. Being a full-time student at a community college is like having a full-time job, with all the pressures (and perhaps even more) that come with it. College can be stressful, particularly for new students. Don't let it overwhelm you. If you spend every waking minute studying and going to classes, you'll burn out quickly and perhaps even drop out. Try to maintain a healthy balance between school and life. Set aside time each day for yourself—for exercise, nonschool reading, socializing with friends, or entertainment. Take care of your body. Eat healthy foods and get plenty of sleep, or at least as much as you can every night. (Pull an all-nighter? Don't even think about it.) Taking steps to manage stress might just be the most important thing you can do for yourself as a full-time community college student.

12

If You're Going to Community College as a Career Changer

Juggling Classes, Homework, Your Job, and the Rest of Your Life

Going to college as a career changer will be a very serious juggling act with consequences not only for you, but for everyone in your life. It will have an impact on children, spouses and partners, other family members, and close friends—and on your relationships with all of them. If you are working while going to school, as most career changers must do, your community college experience could also have a positive or negative impact on your job performance—positive insofar as it improves your skills and confidence, or negative insofar as it stretches you too thin.

Earning a degree or certificate in community college while keeping up with a full range of life, family, and work responsibilities is a huge challenge. If you commit yourself to the process for the long haul, however, you will be able to meet the challenge successfully and achieve your higher education and career goals.

You will probably find that you have a lot of anxiety at the start of your first semester in community college. That's normal. Remember how anxious and excited you were when you started high school. It's only natural that you should be just as anxious and excited, if not more so, when you start college.

The cure for that anxiety is to establish and follow good habits and practices as a student. I've already discussed this in Chapter 9,

"What You Should Do to Prepare for College-Level Work if You're Going to Community College as a Career Changer." Reading that chapter again will be useful as you begin taking courses. You might also take another look at Chapters 8 and 11; although primarily addressed to students coming directly from high school, they have information and tips on preparing for and succeeding in college that are applicable for all students. In particular, don't miss the advice on time management, class attendance, note taking, test taking, study habits, and writing papers in Chapter 11. (Likewise, Chapter 9 and this chapter have information and tips that will be useful for students coming directly from high school as well as career changers.)

The same habits that make for successful preparation for college make for success in college. Don't rush and overload yourself early in the process. Build confidence and take on more challenges as you go. Use your time wisely and don't procrastinate. Engage all the resources at your disposal early and often. Develop and practice good study and assignment habits.

In addition, here are some other important keys for a successful community college experience.

Attend Orientation

Start things off on the right foot by attending orientation. Career changers often mistakenly assume that orientation is mainly about campus life apart from academics, and that this is important only for younger students. Or they think that they can pick up everything they need to know on the fly. Besides, career changers are always pressed for time, and devoting one or more days to orientation can easily seem like a luxury you can't afford. At Ivy Tech orientation is mandatory, but can be attended online.

Participating in orientation activities will save you time in the long run, however. Orientation is a concentrated, one-time opportunity to learn how your community college works as an institution, from academic advising to financial aid, career planning and advising, tutoring services, and counseling and other student services. If you're like most students, recent high school graduates and career changers alike, you're going to need to engage with a variety of college offices and services in every semester. If you attend orientation, you will know where to find them and how to work with them when you need them. You'll be able to navigate your way more efficiently and effectively through all the normal ins and outs of course registration, financial aid, and the like, as well as through any special issues that arise along the way.

Campus services can also help connect you to resources and services that are provided by local community groups or by municipal, state, or federal agencies. Whatever outside issues you're facing as a career changer, from finding good child care to sorting out veterans' benefits, chances are that an office on campus can help you or at least point you in the right direction. Orientation is the best time to learn which college services can help you with such issues.

As I emphasized in Chapter 9, career changers have to guard against trying to be overly self-sufficient in handling the problems that crop up for them as students. They often think that because of their age and life experience, they should be able to handle everything on their own. That's not realistic. Every successful college student needs help of different kinds along the way. Career changers are also often extra-sensitive about asking "dumb" questions. But there really are no dumb questions except for the ones you don't ask.

Remember that the college's administration, faculty, and staff all want you to succeed, and they are glad to see you tapping into college resources and services. Statistics show that the more that students use the resources and services available to them, the more likely they are to succeed in college.

As a career changer you should use all the resources and services available to you, starting with your academic advisor. A good understanding and close working relationship with your academic advisor will be critical to your success in college, beginning with helping you to establish clear academic and career goals and define a plan for achieving them.

Get on Track in the Right Academic and Career Paths

If possible, your preparation for community college should include developing a clear plan for a specific course of study and career goal. As I emphasized in the "Find Your Field and Begin Building Your Support Network" section in Chapter 9, the sooner you can make these decisions, the better.

If you don't have a clear, detailed plan for completing a course of study and achieving your career goal when you start community college, however, make developing that plan an immediate priority. In consultation with your academic advisor and a career planning advisor, follow the "Find Your Field" tips in Chapter 9. Identify a career goal based on your existing skills and interests and on job growth where you live or want to live. Then work backward from that goal to figure out the course of study you need to achieve it.

Make your academic and career plan your template for success, chart your progress on it, and update it regularly. At a minimum, you should review your plan, and revise it as needed, at the beginning and end of every semester with the help of your academic and career advisors.

Make the Most of Your First Semester—and Every Subsequent Semester

More career changers stumble in their first semester because they have overloaded or mismanaged their course schedules than for any other reason. These missteps have become more common because students can now register online and choose courses independently. Eager to get on with their lives and determined not to waste time, career changers often take on too much and wind up crashing and burning. Often they also choose courses that don't really fit their certificate or degree goal.

Don't make course and course load decisions without consulting your academic advisor and perhaps also someone from career services. Academic and career advisors can give you valuable perspective on how to arrange the sequence of courses your certificate or degree program requires. You want to take courses in a way that makes academic sense and that also enables you to build your confidence.

Start your college studies with the courses in your certificate or degree program that you feel most comfortable handling, and then progress to more difficult courses from semester to semester. If you run into trouble keeping up in a course, seek help from the college tutoring service right away. Don't try to catch up simply by intensifying your own efforts. You probably will have to work harder to catch up, but you should work smarter, too, by utilizing any tutoring or other help that is available. If you anticipate that a course is going to challenge you academically, whether it's in the first or a later semester, make contact with campus tutoring in that subject area at the start of the course. This will increase the chances that you can complete the course successfully.

Managing your course load—in your first college semester and subsequent semesters—is also about balancing the demands of different courses against each other. For example, if you take a sociology course, an English course, and a psychology course in the same semester, you will probably have intensive reading and writing to do in all three courses. It might make better sense to substitute a math or science course for one of them, simply to give yourself a change of pace and course work during the semester.

Keep in mind that every college course is a significant time commitment. A good rule of thumb, as I mentioned in Chapters 9 and 11, is 10 hours a week per course, counting both classroom time and study and assignment time. For a full course load of four courses a semester, that's a 40-hour work week. If you happen to be starting your first semester during summer session, you need to budget even more time—15 hours a week per course—because summer courses are accelerated. They condense the normal 16-week-semester course content into 8 or 10 weeks with longer class times and more homework. You should also budget 15 hours a week for especially difficult courses during regular semesters.

Although it may seem like starting too slow, it is a good idea for career changers to take only one or two courses in their first college semester. Get yourself used to being a college student and incorporating its demands into your work and family life. Remember the fable of the tortoise and the hare, and don't be in too big a rush to succeed. Going slow and steady at the start will help you to finish faster and stronger at the end.

Block scheduling of courses can be a great boon to career changers, especially those who are working full time. But beware of trying to cram a full-semester course load into only two days on campus. If you've got four classes on one day, you're bound to become fatigued and inattentive as the day goes on. That's a formula for falling behind in one or more courses. It is easier to take advantage of the convenience of block scheduling when you are taking less than a full course load.

If you are planning on taking courses online, it is often wise to delay doing so until your second semester. Get used to being a college student in regular on-campus courses first. Remember that online courses require more motivation and discipline, and often involve more homework and assignments, than on-campus courses. You also have to be tech savvy enough for online courses, and this is something you can work on improving in your first semester. Again, if you don't overload yourself at the beginning, you will be able to go further and faster in the end.

Career changers who have been placed into remedial courses by their community college may feel like they have lost before they have started. There is no denying that the success rate for students in remediation has been low, although Ivy Tech and other community colleges across the country are making real strides in turning this situation around (see the discussion of remediation in Chapter 10, "The Placement Tests That Determine Where You Start in College"). Keeping your eye on your ultimate goals will help you find the motivation and patience you need to work through remedial courses and advance to college-level work. Remember that taking remedial courses does not indicate that you lack smarts or potential; it only means you aren't yet prepared to use your smarts and develop your potential in college-level courses.

One of the best things you can do during your first semester is to take a student success course. Different colleges use different labels for these courses, which give you practice in study and research skills, writing research papers, and all the other things you need to know and do to succeed in college. For example, such a course will introduce you to whatever electronic course management system your college uses (for more on such systems, see Chapter 7). And it will offer valuable guidance on things like interacting with professors, administrators, and staff, including appropriate protocol for face-to-face meetings and communicating via e-mail. These interactions can and should be friendly—again, faculty and staff want to help you succeed—but they probably will also be a little more formal in some ways than you may be used to. It's better to know the right ways to do these things at the start of your college studies.

A student success course also will help you get comfortable with one other aspect of community college that may be new to you, the tremendous diversity of the student body. As I suggested in Chapter 9, you should treat interacting with students of all ethnicities and from all walks of life as preparation for functioning positively and effectively in today's increasingly diverse workplaces.

It bears repeating one more time that you should not make decisions about registering for courses without consulting your academic advisor and perhaps also someone from career services. That applies to all semesters, but it is especially important during your first semester.

Family Matters

Even if you are well prepared to do college-level work, the time and effort college requires will be a shock to you and your family. You need to cultivate a support system at home and among extended family and friends so they will not resent your devoting huge amounts of time to attending classes, studying and doing assignments, and participating in college-related activities.

As I suggested in Chapter 9, sharing your schedule for classes, studying, and doing assignments is a good way to begin talking with family members about the commitment you are making to college, and how this will benefit you and the whole family over time. Put the schedule on the refrigerator door or kitchen bulletin board, so that everyone knows when you need time to yourself, unless there is an emergency.

Seeing your schedule and knowing when you'll be free to interact can be reassuring for family members who are concerned about getting your attention, especially children. The schedule will give everyone a sense of structure, and help you avoid feeling guilty about the commitment of time and effort that college requires.

Another useful practice is a weekly meeting at which family members can raise their individual and mutual concerns. This should be an occasion to show the rest of the family that you care as much about what each of them is doing and experiencing as you do about your college studies. Of course there will be stresses and strains, sometimes difficult ones, as the family adjusts to your being in college. But there will also be opportunities for the family as a whole, and each of its members, to grow by working together and helping each other achieve positive goals.

Sherron Washington was a junior in high school when she became pregnant. She was determined to finish high school and continue her education so that she could build a better life for her child. A guidance counselor suggested Ivy Tech, and she enrolled as a full-time student while working 40 hours a week as an aide in an assisted living center. "I could never have done this without the support of my family. They helped with childcare and encouraged me every step of the way," she says.

She was interested in the field of criminal justice because she wanted to give something back to her community by guiding children and teenagers through the court system. In 2011, she received an associate's degree in criminal justice. "The most valuable part of my education at Ivy Tech was my internship with the Marion County Probation Department. I learned what it was like to work day to day helping teenagers in trouble," she says.

She is now a junior at Indiana State pursuing a criminal justice major. Her goal is to be a probation officer for juveniles, a career that pays between $30,000 and $60,000 a year.

Family members and friends generally will all want to support you and help you succeed. But they may not know the best way to do so if they have no experience of college and don't know what it involves. Without meaning to, they may wind up undermining, rather than bolstering, your efforts. Or family and friends may fear that your education is making you grow away from them, and may express resentment about that. Unfortunately, students from backgrounds with low income and low educational attainment sometimes unconsciously choose to fail rather than feel that they no longer fit in with their home community and those close to them.

When life problems like these arise, visit your school's student counseling center. At the very least you will find an understanding ear and learn coping skills that have worked for other students in similar situations. That can make all the difference in keeping you on track to succeed and improve your life and that of your family.

Get to Know Professors, Staff, and Fellow Students

Every community college student should also cultivate a support system inside the institution. Your internal support system begins with your academic advisor and should include other members of the college community, from staff in financial aid, career advising, and other offices to instructors and fellow students.

Career changers often look at campus organizations and activities and think, "It'd be nice if I had the time, but I don't." The more you become involved in the life of the community college, however, the richer your experience will be. Statistics also show that the more you do this, the likelier you will be to complete your certificate or degree program. If at all possible, make time for one non–course-related activity with fellow students every week.

Another tendency of career changers is to hold back from approaching their professors and program chairs for one-on-one discussions. They come to campus to attend class, and then immediately leave.

Get to know your professors and program chairs. Visit them during their office hours. Professors and program chairs who know you as a person will be better able to help you advance in your studies and suggest career opportunities, such as internships, that are a good fit for you. Remember that there is no such thing as a dumb question where these folks are concerned, and that they will be eager to help you find your way to success.

Likewise, fellow students can be a great resource for academic and social support. In this regard, you should be aware that younger students will often look to you and other career changers for classroom leadership and real-world experience. Your professors will often do this as well. Appreciate that you have a lot to offer your fellow students and others in the campus community, and draw motivation and strength from that.

Make time to attend campus workshops and other programs that interest you. Career services and other student services will put on many valuable workshops and programs throughout the year. These are great opportunities to connect with other students and learn about ways to enhance your education and your career preparation.

Job Issues

If it is possible financially, consider working less while you are in college so that you can devote more energy to your studies. But don't be a full-time student simply to max out your financial aid. As I've said, overloading yourself academically is a bad strategy.

If you're looking for work, plan your course schedule around when you expect to be working after you find a job. That may mean working days and going to school at night, or the other way around, but it's not something you can change in the middle of a semester.

Those of you who work for large companies may be able to draw on professional development programs that your employer offers. Such programs may include some flexibility in working hours or even provide funds to help you pay for community college. If there is no formal program to encourage and support workers who are seeking additional education and career enhancement, you might still be able to find a mentor at your job who can become part of your external support system and help you stay on track to achieve your goals.

■ ■ ■

Two students who exemplify success in community college as career changers are Chrystal Boston and Michael Rice, both African Americans from low-income backgrounds.

In the spring of 2007, Chrystal was a divorced mother with a five-year-old daughter and a three-year-old son, and she was working as a waitress at one of the Indianapolis locations of the O'Charley's restaurant chain. Several of her coworkers were Ivy Tech students. Eager to do something in life besides wait tables, she investigated attending Ivy Tech herself and decided to enroll.

Chrystal began taking classes at Ivy Tech–Indianapolis in the 2007 summer session, but a few weeks after the start of the session she discovered she was pregnant. Unsure whether she could stay in school during her pregnancy and the new child's infancy, while also looking after her five- and three-year-olds, even with her mother's help with childcare, she dropped her summer session courses.

But with her mother's support, Chrystal decided that it did not make sense to delay her studies, and she registered for a full course load in the fall 2007 semester. Chrystal says, "My mom is truly my role model. She is the backbone of our family, and I learned my sense of hard work and dedication to a goal from her."

Being pregnant meant one significant change to Chrystal's educational plans, however. She had intended to emulate one of her friends at O'Charley's and become a nurse. But because she was pregnant, she couldn't expose herself to formaldehyde and similar substances that she would encounter in nursing classes. She tried business classes instead, and found she loved them.

Chrystal had her third child, a boy, in February of 2008. She says, "He was due on Valentine's Day. But he decided to come a little early, and he arrived on Groundhog Day." After six weeks, she was back taking a full course load. She continued to take a full course load in the 2008 summer session and the following two semesters, graduating with an associate's degree in business administration in May of 2009.

Along the way she became president of the Ivy Tech–Indianapolis student government association, achieved a 4.0 GPA, became a member of Phi Theta Kappa, the community college academic honor society, and wrote a regular blog for the *Indianapolis Star* newspaper's website, all while meeting her responsibilities to her children and working frequent temporary jobs on and off campus. After graduating from Ivy Tech, she transferred to Indiana University–Purdue University–Indianapolis (IUPUI), enrolling in the Purdue School of Engineering and Technology. She was a full-time student at IUPUI at first, but then shifted to going to school part-time so that she could take a full-time job as executive administrative assistant to the head of enrollment management and student affairs at Indianapolis's Martin University.

She is now on track to receive her bachelor's degree in May of 2013, and then intends to pursue a master's degree in public affairs.

For his part Michael Rice graduated high school in the spring of 2002, and then worked at Best Buy for a year so that he could move away from home while attending college. "My relationship with my family was and is strong," Michael says. "But I knew I needed a more stable environment to succeed in college." Michael enrolled at Ivy Tech–Muncie in the fall semester of 2002, intending to transfer to a bachelor's program at Ball State University.

But life intervened when he fell in love and began a family. With his first child, a son, on the way, he stopped taking classes after the spring 2004 semester and went to work full time. A little more than a year later his family had grown to include a second child, a daughter. After juggling a number of part-time and temporary full-time jobs, Michael became a teller at an Indianapolis bank, thanks in part to a lead from Ivy Tech–Indianapolis's careers office. He did well at the bank and earned several promotions, but he lost his job in the recession and the resulting financial turmoil also took a toll on his relationship with his children's mother. After the relationship ended, the children lived with their mother, but Michael continued to be an involved, committed father.

In the spring of 2009 he resumed his college studies by enrolling at Ivy Tech–Indianapolis. But he started slowly with only one course—an economics class. Michael says, "I knew I had to get acclimated to being a college student again. I also knew I needed to develop a support system within Ivy Tech, beginning with my academic advisor and transfer advisor. Now that I was back in school, I still wanted to transfer to a bachelor's degree program."

Michael got an A in that first economics course. He took two courses in the 2009 summer session, excelling in both of them. A scholarship from the Nina Mason Pulliam Charitable Trust enabled him to become a full-time student in the fall semester of 2009. Like Chrystal, he won admission to Phi Theta Kappa. He completed his associate's degree in business administration in May 2011, and transferred seamlessly to IUPUI, enrolling in the undergraduate division of Indiana University's Kelley School of Business. By working closely with transfer advisors at both Ivy Tech and IUPUI, Michael was able to transfer a whopping 74 credits—the normal maximum is 62 to 64 credits—to his bachelor's degree program at the Kelley School of Business. He is on track to complete his bachelor's degree in May of 2013 with a triple major in business administration, human resources, and international business. I was proud to have Michael accompany me to the first ever White House Summit on Community Colleges on October 5, 2010.

Keeping on track in community college can be hard for any student. As a career changer you have even more going on in your life, more daily demands and potential crises and distractions, than the average student coming directly from high school. In this regard, remember that the most important element to success as a community college student is remaining true to your dream. Keep your goal in mind, keep working hard, and like Chrystal Boston and Michael Rice, you will succeed.

Conclusion

Nothing can hide the fact that community college is the smart higher education choice for increasing numbers of students. As we've seen in this book, professional certificates and associate's degrees have become the favored gateways to many of today's and tomorrow's best jobs. And two years at community college have become a viable alternative to the first two years of a bachelor's degree program at a four-year college or university.

In fact, there is no evidence that going to an elite school for a bachelor's degree offers any guarantee of future success. Conversely, there is strong evidence that community college can accelerate four-year bachelor's degree attainment and/or quickly put you on a desirable career path. A two-year graduate from a community college transferring to a four-year school has better odds to complete a bachelor's degree in two more years (four years total) than a student who enters the same four-year school as a freshman. And Anthony Carnevale and colleagues' research at the Georgetown University Center on Education and the Workforce clearly shows that those who complete a one-year certificate or two-year degree at community college in a variety of STEM and health care–related occupational areas can often outearn four-year college graduates.

Meanwhile, the money available to borrow in the form of student loans has become a siren song that has stranded, and is still stranding, far too many people and their families on the financial rocks—perhaps for their whole lives and even subsequent generations. On a personal level the results can be tragic, as I have unfortunately seen up close. The impact on our society is also extreme.

The ripple effect of student loan debt means that the traditional four-year college experience has become unaffordable, not only for all but the most affluent Americans, but for the country as a whole.

So what can parents do to provide the higher education their children need for a good life? What can career changers do to obtain the higher education they need to improve life for themselves and their families?

Two years of community college will save $40,000 to $50,000 of four-year college costs. Think of saving or investing that money for the long-term future, or using it for a house, a car, or two years of graduate or professional school.

Whether you are intent on earning a bachelor's degree and possibly higher degrees as well, or a professional certificate or associate's degree that qualifies you in a high-demand field, think of achieving your American dream without a mountain of debt.

Not for the first time in the nation's history, the American dream stands in need of reinvention and renewal. The process of reinventing and renewing the American dream will be a complicated one with many elements, but there is no doubt that community colleges will remain at the center of the story over the years ahead. I hope this book will play a useful role in furthering that process, and will help you achieve your educational, career, and life goals.

Appendix
The Higher Education
America Needs

Win-Win Partnerships Between Community Colleges and Employers

As is customary on such occasions, President Barack Obama took some time during his 2012 State of the Union address to introduce several people in the audience to the nation. Some in the media and the business community were surprised that one of those people was a career changer who got workforce retraining at a community college. To quote President Obama, "Jackie Bray is a single mom from North Carolina who was laid off from her job as a mechanic. Then Siemens opened a gas turbine factory in Charlotte, and formed a partnership with Central Piedmont Community College. The company helped the college design courses in laser and robotics training. . . . [They] paid Jackie's tuition, then hired her to help operate their plant."

The vital role of community colleges in workforce training and retraining should come as no surprise to savvy businesses of all sizes. Jackie Bray's story represents the stories of tens of thousands of workers who begin to train or retrain for highly skilled jobs at community colleges every year.

As I've repeated throughout this book, America's community colleges are a unique national resource. Many countries are facing skill gaps in their workforces during these troubled economic times. Yet no other nation has a resource quite like our community colleges. The over 1,000 community colleges across America all feature worker training as a core element of their reason for being and ongoing mission. In fact, the community colleges are educating almost as many students in worker training programs off campus as the seven million students on campus.

In the rest of this book I've been speaking primarily to students and their families. Chapters 4, 6, and 7, which respectively discuss STEM careers, two-year degrees and one-year professional certificates, and online studies, emphasize the value of business—community college partnerships for those seeking both immediate "learn and earn" opportunities and preparation for great jobs and careers. Guaranteed jobs, free tuition, wages for study, and training for hot industries are just some of the benefits that business—community college partnerships provide to students and working learners.

Here I'd like to speak primarily to business, community, and government leaders (prospective students and their families, as well as guidance counselors, will also find useful information in what follows). If you are not yet fostering partnerships with community colleges to supply the highly skilled workers that business and economic growth demand, you should be.

Community colleges are the most flexible, cost-effective tool you can find for workforce training and retraining. They boast an unrivalled ability to develop courses that meet the dual needs of college credit on the one hand and workplace knowledge and skill development on the other.

Community college and business partnerships are true win-win relationships. Actually, they're win-win-win relationships that benefit whole communities and regions as well as the businesses and community colleges involved. Advantages for companies include reduced total training costs, improved employee retention, fewer accidents, less rework, and increased productivity and profit. Advantages for community colleges include better opportunities for their students, improved program completion and graduation rates, and increased revenue that helps the colleges fulfill their educational mission despite freezes and cuts in government funding. Advantages for local communities and states include economic growth; a healthier tax base; and large savings in the form of avoided health care, criminal justice, welfare, and unemployment costs. All these positive results flow from having better educated, more highly skilled, more productive—and consequently better-paid—workers.

Taken as a whole, the business–community college partnerships around the country contribute hugely to the nation's economic recovery. As the case studies below indicate, there is potential for even greater contributions to our economic growth and prosperity in the years ahead.

Ivy Tech has developed partnerships with companies such as $18 billion global engine and diversified machinery manufacturer Cummins, steel maker ArcelorMittal, and drug manufacturer Cook Pharmica, among others. You need senior leaders on both sides to play active roles if you want such associations to succeed, and for Ivy Tech and Cummins, respectively, those leaders are John Hogan, chancellor of Ivy Tech's Columbus campus, and Mark Gerstle, vice president and chief administrative officer at Cummins. As president of Ivy Tech I have direct involvement, and so does Cummins CEO Tom Linebarger. But having senior leaders like John Hogan and Mark Gerstle running the show day to day is vital to its success.

Together, Ivy Tech and Cummins have developed a manufacturing skills curriculum that we can customize for each of a dozen Cummins plants across the United States. Students can apply the course credits in this curriculum to an associate of applied science degree that represents additional value to the company. Cummins employees and prospective employees now study together at the Columbus Learning Center, a joint venture of Ivy Tech–Columbia and Indiana University–Purdue University–Columbus (IUPUC), which physically links our campuses. The next phase—one that's already in motion—is for Cummins and Ivy Tech to take this curriculum to the company's plants overseas in China and elsewhere.

Likewise, Ivy Tech's East Chicago campus is working with ArcelorMittal to prepare the steelworkers of the future. Arcelor-Mittal's director of education, Mark Langbehn, knows that the company needs 400 new employees a year with an associate's degree in industrial technology. A high school diploma can now serve as a good start to a well-paid career in the steel industry, if it is soon accompanied by an associate's degree.

Another important partnership for Ivy Tech is with Indiana's joint apprenticeship program in skilled trades, including electrical, iron, mill, and sheet metal work, operating systems engineering, elevator construction, plumbing and pipe fitting, and teledata technology. Every year a thousand new students enter this "learn and earn" program, which combines the four- to five-year path to a journeyman's certificate in one of the trades with completion of an associate of applied science degree.

Community colleges across the nation are doing similarly exciting things: partnering with businesses, trade associations, and government in order to generate big dividends for students, businesses, and local economies. What follows is just a sample.

Test Flight: An Aerospace Training Program Takes Students to New Heights

There are more than 650 aerospace companies in Washington State, which makes it the nation's king of airplane building. Yet a workforce that's going gray quickly has industry leaders worried the crown could slip. Three-quarters of the aerospace factory workers in Washington will be eligible for retirement within the next decade or so. Half of the workforce at Boeing alone will reach retirement age within just five years.[1]

So who's going to step into those jobs when replacements are needed? Thanks to a unique partnership begun in the summer of 2010, graduates of Edmonds Community College in Lynnwood,

Washington, will have a leg up. The college has teamed up with the Aerospace Futures Alliance of Washington—an industry group of companies such as Boeing, Bombardier, and Embraer—to open the Washington Aerospace Training & Research Center. Operating out of a former aerospace plant, the center mixes lab work and hands-on training to teach skills from riveting to drilling into titanium. At the industry's request, it offers an accelerated program that allows students—some of whom have never even worked with tools before—to earn certificates in just 12 weeks.

The center is quickly creating the pipeline of skilled workers that the industry desperately needs. Its first graduating class saw 80 percent of students land a job in the field.[2] The center is doubling its physical plant in order to enroll more students—and produce more workers for aerospace companies that are crucial to the state's economic health. As two local workforce development leaders point out, "This public–private partnership is a perfect example of the way industry can lead the way for workforce training—training that ends in jobs."[3]

Kentucky and UPS Create a Program That Delivers

In late 1997, Kentucky was facing an economic disaster. Package-handling juggernaut United Parcel Service (UPS) was threatening to move its cargo airline from Louisville, where it had been based since the company first began offering next-day delivery in 1982.[4] UPS wanted to double its package-handling capacity at the Louisville airport, but there weren't enough qualified part-time workers in the metropolitan area. Company officials explained that without a bigger labor pool, they would be forced to pull up stakes and shift the air cargo operation out of the state.

On Christmas Eve, higher education leaders in Kentucky delivered to then-Governor Paul Patton a proposal to avert the crisis.[5] Following this proposal, the University of Louisville and two area community colleges jointly founded Metropolitan College, or "Metro," as it's known. This wasn't a new school; rather, it was a program to give part-time UPS workers a free education. Now 14 years old, the program has attracted thousands of workers to UPS, prevented a job-loss catastrophe for Louisville, and become a national model of workforce training.

Here's how it works. Anyone who signs on as a package handler on the night shift of UPS's overnight air operation is eligible to enroll in the Metro program through either the University of Louisville or Jefferson Community & Technical College (the school that emerged from the merger of the two community colleges that started the program). Classes are held at times that fit the students' work schedules, with some hosted at a UPS facility.

Metro uses state and local funding to cover half the tuition cost for students, while UPS picks up the tab for the rest. The worker-students earn a regular hourly wage for their shift work, plus full-time benefits, including health insurance. UPS also reimburses workers for some textbook costs and pays bonuses of anywhere from $575 to $2,350 when students reach certain academic milestones.

This unusual combination of pay and benefits has helped draw workers to UPS—and students to higher education. Metro opened with nearly 800 students in July 1998, and now enrolls close to 2,000 annually. The program has been a boon to Kentucky, where less than a third of young adults have a college degree—one of the lowest rates in the country.[6] Metro attracts students from all over the state and even a handful from outside Kentucky. Many of them are nontraditional students who couldn't go to college without the free tuition and the class schedule adjusted to accommodate their job. Some are the first members of their families to go to college.

UPS, meanwhile, has tapped the program to reduce worker turnover and boost the size and quality of its labor force. Average employee tenure for UPS part-time workers has increased from just eight weeks at the time Metropolitan College opened to nearly two years today. The company now runs one of most efficient air hubs in the country; estimates suggest it has achieved a 600 percent return on its investment in the students.[7]

It's a win-win-win for Louisville, UPS, and the state. "There's no catch," says Mitch Nichols, president of UPS's airline division. "UPS needs a healthy, vibrant Louisville. The students are motivated to be successful."[8]

The program has become a national model for how private–public partnerships can spur economic development and increase graduation rates. In 2000, the U.S. Department of Labor gave it an award as an innovative solution to workforce development, and it's being touted by the Obama administration as a model of so-called learn-and-earn training. And other companies—including Pacific Gas and Electric, Gap, and McDonald's—have expressed interest in creating similar programs of their own.[9]

Meanwhile, Metropolitan College has expanded to train workers for the health care company Humana and elder home health care provider ResCare. Like UPS, both companies have established tuition-assistance programs through Metropolitan for their workers.

Fine Wines and Good Jobs in Washington State

In 2011, Walla Walla Community College was named one of the five best community colleges in the nation by the Aspen Institute's College Excellence Program. The rural eastern Washington school was chosen for its general excellence, including graduation and transfer-to-four-year-school rates that are well above the national average and a good track record with minority students. But the Aspen judges were particularly struck by how school administrators and faculty were so tightly connected to employers. The college had become a keen analyst of the local job market's past and present—and, more important, its future.

"They're not just responding to current needs," says Josh Wynder, director of Aspen's program. "They're studying the trends and making judgments about what the future will be."

One of Walla Walla's key partners is Economic Modeling Specialists Inc. (EMSI), a regional consulting firm that provides the college with projected employment data that's so fine grained it can even detail specific job titles that will see a boom in coming years. Such forward-looking analysis has been critical as the region's once-strong lumber and food-processing industries have faded. The school is "about inventing the future," says Egils Milbergs, executive director of the Washington Economic Development Commission.[10]

The best example of what's emerged from this forward thinking is the college's Center for Enology and Viticulture. Begun in 2001 with the goal of supplying workers for what was then only a handful of wineries, the center focuses on teaching students the intricacies of irrigation, pest control, fermentation, pressing, and bottling. Along the way, the center opened its own winery, College Cellars, so that students could learn every aspect of the winery business. In addition to studying the art and science of winemaking, the students perform all the tasks involved in it. They dig holes for grapevine trestles, drive forklifts, and sterilize fermentation tanks.

More than a decade after the center opened, there are some 140 wineries in the region. Walla Walla alumni staff many of them, and some have even started their own businesses. The boom in wine has reversed the fortunes of the area, which is enjoying a new cachet as the Napa Valley of Washington State. The many local wineries draw increasing numbers of tourists and support the expansion of tourism-related businesses such as restaurants and hotels. According to EMSI, the number of jobs in what it calls "wine cluster" industries climbed from 283 in 1997 to more than 3,200 10 years later. By 2017, that number will double, and wine-related jobs will account for 16 percent of all jobs in the region.[11]

North Carolina's Apprenticeship Program: College for Free—and a Paycheck

Faced with a new problem in workforce training, a North Carolina community college is teaming up with business on an old-fashioned solution. Once the hothouse of the nation's textile industry, North

Carolina is now seeing fast growth in advanced manufacturing. Yet many of the companies in this industry can't find the skilled workers they need to run their sophisticated machinery.

In order to prime the pump and increase the pool of skilled manufacturing workers, Central Piedmont Community College partnered with manufacturers to launch a new training program in 1995. Known as Apprenticeship 2000, the program is modeled after apprenticeships found in trades throughout Europe for hundreds of years. Participants are typically high school students or young adults. The companies pay their way at Central Piedmont, where they take math and classes in computer and technical skills. At the same time, the students apprentice at the participating companies, getting trade-specific skills as well as an hourly wage.[12]

Apprenticeship 2000 graduates earn an associate's degree and a guaranteed job in the field, with a minimum starting salary of $34,000 a year. One of the first companies in the program, Blum Inc., a homegrown hardware fabricator, has a $1.8 million training facility and three instructors dedicated to teaching the apprentices.

Thanks to his hands-on role in building Apprenticeship 2000 and similar programs, Dr. Tony Zeiss, Central Piedmont's president for more than 20 years, has become a recognized leader in creating and running successful business–community college partnerships. Tony grew up in Arcadia, Indiana, and he has been an invaluable mentor to me in this area since my rookie year as a community college president in 2007.

The most recent of the eight companies to participate in Apprenticeship 2000 (the others, besides Blum, are Ameritech, Chiron, Daetwyler, Pfaff, Sarstedt, and Timken) is Siemens Corporation, the American subsidiary of the German engineering conglomerate. I already mentioned Siemens's new gas turbine factory in Charlotte in connection with retrained worker Jackie Bray's attendance at President Obama's 2012 State of the Union address. As the nation's biggest gas turbine plant, the Siemens factory will need hundreds of workers with precision machining skills in the coming years. Much of the current workforce is eligible for retirement, and Siemens executives worry that attrition will hurt their growth. The company is investing upwards of $165,000 per student in the apprentice program, but expects a big payoff. "We're just not finding the people we need out in the market," says Eric Spiegel, president and CEO of Siemens in America. "We need to create them."[13]

As one working learner, Estevan Torres, explains, "It's basically your life plan set out for you. They pay for your education, and a job is waiting."[14]

Here are a few other partnerships between community colleges and businesses that offer promise for students and the economy:

- The shipbuilding facilities of Northrop Grumman in Newport News, Virginia, offer a "co-op" program to Thomas Nelson Community College students who major in computer-aided drafting and design or mechanical engineering technology. Students attend classes for free while they are paid to work and train at Northrop.
- Leading agricultural machinery manufacturer John Deere pays the tuition of students at Southeast Community College in Milford, Nebraska, who are pursuing associate's degrees in applied sciences and aiming to work as technicians at the company's dealerships. As part of its 23-year-old partnership with the school, John Deere also supplies equipment, trucks, and tractors to Southeast to further the students' training.
- Tyler Junior College in Tyler, Texas, is home to a corporate training academy for local power company Luminant, which puts up more than $175,000 a year for scholarships to students on the path to earning an associate's degree in power plant technology.
- Freeport-McMoRan Copper & Gold Inc., an international mining company based in Phoenix, Arizona, offers full scholarships and paid internships to qualified students at Yavapai College who are studying diesel, industrial plant, or electrical technology.

- The biotech industry in Ohio is working with six state two-year schools—Owens Community College, Cuyahoga Community College, Lakeland Community College, Columbus State Community College, Cincinnati State Technical and Community College, and Sinclair Community College—to provide training for workers who have been displaced from automotive, manufacturing, and other declining industries. The training will prepare students for entry-level tech positions in the biotech and pharmaceutical fields.
- Also in Ohio, the Health Careers Collaborative of Greater Cincinnati, a partnership managed by Cincinnati State Technical and Community College, prepares students for jobs at Cincinnati Children's Hospital and at hospitals and physician clinics in southwestern Ohio and neighboring regions of Kentucky.

Government naturally has a role to play in supporting business–community college partnerships. One very significant example of this is the National Science Foundation's funding of advanced technological education centers (ATECs) across the country, which I've already discussed in Chapter 4. Designed to boost our STEM workforce, the ATEC program currently includes 36 centers in advanced manufacturing technologies; biotechnology and chemical processes; electronics, micro-, and nanotechnologies; engineering technologies; and information, geospatial, and cyber-security technologies.

Each ATEC has a lead community college partner and one or more major business partners. For example, the Automotive Manufacturing Technical Education Collaborative is led from the community college side by the Kentucky Community and Technical College System. Participating companies include Toyota, BMW, Ford, General Motors, and major automotive suppliers. The program is not confined to Kentucky, but includes community colleges in Alabama, Indiana (Ivy Tech), Michigan, Mississippi, Ohio, Tennessee, and Texas.

Local and regional workforce investment boards that were created to implement the federal Workforce Investment Act of 1998 are another important channel for developing business–community college partnerships in worker training. Every year these boards funnel federal funds (over $2 billion in 2011) to workforce training programs. Every county and major town or city has such a board, and the county executive or city mayor appoints its members. At least half of the workforce investment must be from the private sector, with other members representing community colleges, labor unions, and community groups. (For more on these boards, visit the website of the National Association of Workforce Boards, www.nawb.org.)

As I travel to Ivy Tech's 30 campuses throughout Indiana, businesspeople tell me over and over again that key positions will remain unfilled without targeted workforce training. My message to them, and to businesspeople around the country, is simple. Community colleges will be eager, capable, and low-cost partners for you. But you must take an active lead in the process.

Successful companies like the ones I've highlighted know that they cannot wait for qualified workers to show up at their door. You can't do that, either. You should have the direct office numbers of community college administrators on your own office phone's speed dial, and their mobile phone numbers on your own mobile phone. They most likely already have a successful track record in workforce training and retraining, and can share best-practice models with you. You should get to know your local workforce investment board. And you can also find best-practice examples and case studies through the National Association of Workforce Boards and the organization Corporate Voices for Working Families (www.cvworkingfamilies.org).

In these deficit-challenged times, community colleges are making an enormous contribution to economic recovery through workforce training. We stretch limited private and public workforce training funds to achieve impressive returns for our students, our business partners, and our communities and states. Together, community colleges, businesses, and government are renewing the American dream for tens of thousands of working learners every year. The need is even greater than that. But if we all commit to expanding business–community college partnerships, we can meet that need, and in so doing, put the country's economy on a new growth trajectory.

Appendix
Additional Resources

FINANCIAL AID SITES

Federal Information Page on Pell Grants
http://www2.ed.gov/programs/fpg/index.html

Free Application for Federal Student Aid
http://www.fafsa.ed.gov

Parent Loan for Undergraduate Students
http://studentaid.ed.gov/PORTALSWebApp/students/english/
parentloans.jsp

College Cost Calculator
http://www.collegesavings.org/collegeCostCalculator.aspx

GI Bill
http://www.gibill.va.gov

Federal Supplemental Educational Opportunity Grant
http://www.fseog.com

Teacher Education Assistance for College and Higher Education
http://studentaid.ed.gov/PORTALSWebApp/students/english/
TEACH.jsp

Leveraging Education Assistance Programs
http://www2.ed.gov/programs/leap/index.html

Ford Direct Loans (formerly known as Stafford Loans)
http://www.direct.ed.gov

Perkins Loans
http://www2.ed.gov/programs/fpl/index.html

Federal Work Study
http://www2.ed.gov/programs/fws/index.html

College Goal Sunday
http://www.collegegoalsundayusa.org

National Student Loan Data System
http://www.nslds.ed.gov/nslds_SA

College Board
http://www.collegeboard.org

Center on Education and the Workforce—Georgetown University
http://cew.georgetown.edu

TRANSFERRING TO A FOUR-YEAR COLLEGE OR UNIVERSITY

CollegeFish.org
http://www.collegefish.org

BigFuture
http://www.bigfuture.collegeboard.org

COMMUNITY COLLEGE PLACEMENT TEST PREPARATION

College Board ACCUPLACER Test for Entrance to Community
   Colleges
http://www.collegeboard.com/student/testing/accuplacer

ACT COMPASS Test for Entrance to Community Colleges
http://www.act.org/compass

Educational Opportunity Centers
http://www2.ed.gov/programs/trioeoc/index.html

Khan Academy
http://www.Khanacademy.org

Purple Math
http://www.purplemath.com

DUAL ENROLLMENT PROGRAMS

The list below is a sampling of what is available. Begin your search with community colleges in your own area.

University of Oregon
http://admissions.uoregon.edu/freshmen/dualenrollment

University of Washington—Tacoma
http://www.tacoma.uw.edu/admissions/dual-enrollment-program

Texas A&M University, Blinn College
http://blinnteam.tamu.edu

New York University Community College Transfer Opportunity Program
http://steinhardt.nyu.edu/cctop

Iowa State University Admissions Partnership Program
http://www.admissions.iastate.edu/partnership

The University of North Carolina at Chapel Hill
http://admissions.unc.edu/Apply/Transfer_Students/Transferring_Courses.html

Indiana State University and Ivy Tech Community College
http://www.indstate.edu/transfer/ivytech/

Community College of Philadelphia
http://www.ccp.edu/site/prospective/dual_admissions

Portland Community College, Oregon
http://www.pcc.edu/admissions/dual

SCHOLARSHIPS FOR COMMUNITY COLLEGE STUDENTS

The list below is a sampling of what is available. Remember to search online for scholarships that may be targeted for students with your particular background, interests, or other characteristics.

Hispanic Scholarship Fund
http://www.hsf.net/default.aspx

Scholarships4Students
http://www.scholarships4students.com/scholarships_by_community_college.htm

Foundation for California Community Colleges
http://foundationccc.org/WhatWeDo/ScholarshipEndowment/tabid/361/Default.aspx

CollegeScholarships.org
http://www.collegescholarships.org/grants

Financial Aid Finder
http://www.financialaidfinder.com/student-scholarship-search/community-college-scholarships

Phi Theta Kappa Community College Honor Society—
  Scholarships to Four-Year Institutions
http://www.ptk.org

Sallie Mae Fund Scholarships
http://www.thesalliemaefund.org/smfnew/scholarship/index.html

Asian & Pacific Islander American Scholarship Fund
http://www.apiasf.org

Coca-Cola Scholars Foundation
https://www.coca-colascholars.org

Jack Kent Cooke Foundation
http://www.jkcf.org

Advanced Technological Education Centers

For information on the National Science Foundation's Advanced Technological Education Program, visit www.atecenters.org. Or follow the links below to the 36 individual centers and their lead community college or other postsecondary institutions (in a few cases the lead postsecondary institution for a center is a four-year school, but the programs are still primarily for students from regional community colleges).

Advanced Manufacturing Technologies

- Automotive Manufacturing Technical Education Collaborative (AMTEC, www.autoworkforce.org), Kentucky Community and Technical College System, Versailles, Kentucky
- Center for Advanced Automotive Technology (CAAT, www.macomb.edu/CAAT), Macomb Community College, Warren, Michigan
- Consortium for Alabama Regional Center for Automotive Manufacturing (CARCAM, www.carcam.org), Gadsden State Community College, Gadsden, Alabama
- Florida Advanced Technological Education Center (FLATE, www.fl-ate.org), Hillsborough Community College, Tampa, Florida
- National Center for Manufacturing Education (NCME, www.ncmeresource.org), Sinclair Community College, Dayton, Ohio
- National Center for Rapid Technologies (RapidTech, www.rapidtech.org), Saddleback College, Mission Viejo, California
- Regional Center for Next Generation Manufacturing (RCNGM, www.nextgenmfg.org), Connecticut Community Colleges' College of Technology, Hartford, Connecticut
- Technology and Innovation in Manufacturing and Engineering (TIME Center, www.time-center.org), Community College of Baltimore County, Baltimore County, Maryland
- National Center for Welding Education and Training (Weld-Ed, www.weld-ed.org), Lorain County Community College, Elyria, Ohio

Agricultural, Energy, and Environmental Technologies

- National Resource Center for Agriscience and Technology Education (AgrowKnowledge, www.agroknow.org), Kirkwood Community College, Cedar Rapids, Iowa
- Advanced Technology Environmental and Energy Center (ATEEC, www.ateec.org), Eastern Iowa Community College District, Bettendorf, Iowa
- California Regional Consortium for Engineering Advances in Technological Education (CREATE, www.create-california.org), College of the Canyons, Santa Clarita, California
- Northwest Center for Sustainable Resources (NCSR, www.ncsr.org), Chemeteka Community College, Salem, Oregon
- Viticulture and Enology Science and Technology Alliance (VESTA, www.vesta-usa.org), Missouri State University, Springfield, Missouri

Biotechnology and Chemical Processes

- Next Generation National ATE Center for Biotechnology and Life Sciences (Bio-Link, www.bio-link.org), City College of San Francisco, San Francisco, California
- Center for the Advancement of Process Technology (CAPT, www.captech.org), College of the Mainland, Texas City, Texas
- Northeast Biomanufacturing Center and Collaborative (NBC^2, www.biomanufacturing.org), Montgomery County Community College, Blue Bell, Pennsylvania
- National Network for Pulp and Paper Technology Training (npt^2, www.npt2.org), Alabama Southern Community College, Thomasville, Alabama

Electronics, Micro- and Nanotechnologies

- MATEC Networks National Resource Center (MATEC Networks, www.matecnetworks.org), Maricopa Community Colleges, Phoenix, Arizona

- National Center for Nanotechnology Applications and Career Knowledge (NACK, www.nano4me.org), Penn State University, University Park, Pennsylvania
- Midwest Regional Center for Nanotechnology Education (Nano-Link, www.nano-link.org), Dakota County Technical College, Rosemount, Minnesota
- Northeast Advanced Technological Education Center (NEATEC, www.rcsne.org), Hudson Valley Community College, Troy, New York
- Southwest Center for Microsystems Education (SCME, www.scme-nm.org), University of New Mexico, Albuquerque, New Mexico

Engineering Technologies

- Marine Advanced Technology Education Center (MATE, www.marinetech.org), Monterey Peninsula College, Monterey, California
- National Resource Center for Materials Technology Education (MatEd, www.materialseducation.org), Edmonds Community College, Lynnwood, Washington
- National Center for Optics and Photonics Education (OP-TEC, www.op-tec.org), University of Central Florida, Waco, Texas
- Southeast Maritime and Transportation Center (SMART, www.maritime-technology.org), Tidewater Community College, Virginia Beach, Virginia
- National Resource Center for Aerospace Technical Education (SpaceTEC, www.spacetec.org), Brevard Community College, Cocoa, Florida

Information, Geospatial, and Security Technologies

- Boston Area Advanced Technological Education Connections (BATEC, www.batec.org), University of Massachusetts—Boston, Boston, Massachusetts

- Cyber Security Education Consortium (CSEC, www.csecon line.org), University of Tulsa, Tulsa, Oklahoma
- National Resource Center for Systems Security and Information Assurance (CSSIA, www.cssia.org), Moraine Valley Community College, Palos Hills, Illinois
- Convergence Technology Center (CTC, www.greenITcenter .org), Collin College, Frisco, Texas
- CyberWatch Center (CyberWatch, www.cyberwatchcenter .org), Prince George's Community College, Largo, Maryland
- National Geospatial Technology Center of Excellence (Geo-Tech Center, www.geotechcenter.org), Del Mar College, Corpus Christi, Texas
- Information and Communications Technologies Center (ICT Center, www.ictcenter.org), Springfield Technical Community College, Springfield, Massachusetts
- Mid-Pacific ICT Center (MPICT, www.mpict.org), City College of San Francisco, San Francisco, California

Appendix
Accuplacer® Sample Test

This sample test will help you prepare for the placement tests that community colleges give to entering students. For more information on these placement tests, see Chapter 10, "The Placement Tests That Determine Where You Start in College."

Sentence Skills

In an ACCUPLACER® placement test, there are 20 Sentence Skills questions of two types.

- The first type is sentence correction questions that require an understanding of sentence structure. These questions ask you to choose the most appropriate word or phrase for the underlined portion of the sentence.

- The second type is construction shift questions. These questions ask that a sentence be rewritten according to the criteria shown while maintaining essentially the same meaning as the original sentence.

ACCUPLACER®, AP®, and SAT® are registered trademarks of the College Board. PSAT/NMSQT® is a registered trademark of the College Board and the National Merit Scholarship Corporation. Use of these marks does not imply any affiliation or endorsement of this book by the College Board and National Merit Scholarship Corporation.

Within these two primary categories, the questions are also classified according to the skills being tested. Some questions deal with the logic of the sentence, others with whether or not the answer is a complete sentence, and still others with the relationship between coordination and subordination.

Sentence Skills Sample Questions

Direction for questions 1−5

Select the best version of the underlined part of the sentence. The first choice is the same as the original sentence. If you think the original sentence is best, choose the first answer.

1. Stamp collecting <u>being a hobby that is</u> sometimes used in the schools to teach economics and social studies.
   - A. being a hobby that is
   - B. is a hobby because it is
   - C. which is a hobby
   - D. is a hobby

2. <u>Knocked sideways, the statue looked</u> as if it would fall.
   - A. Knocked sideways, the statue looked
   - B. The statue was knocked sideways, looked
   - C. The statue looked knocked sideways
   - D. The statue, looking knocked sideways,

3. <u>To walk, biking, and driving</u> are Pat's favorite ways of getting around.
   - A. To walk, biking, and driving
   - B. Walking, biking, and driving
   - C. To walk, biking, and to drive
   - D. To walk, to bike, and also driving

4. <u>When you cross the street in the middle of the block, this</u> is an example of jaywalking.

   A. When you cross the street in the middle of the block, this

   B. You cross the street in the middle of the block, this

   C. Crossing the street in the middle of the block

   D. The fact that you cross the street in the middle of the **block**

5. Walking by the corner the other day, <u>a child, I noticed, was watching</u> for the light to change.

   A. a child, I noticed, was watching

   B. I noticed a child watching

   C. a child was watching, I noticed,

   D. there was, I noticed, a child watching

Direction for questions 6–10

Rewrite the sentence in your head following the directions given below. Keep in mind that your new sentence should be well written and should have essentially the same meaning as the original sentence.

6. It is easy to carry solid objects without spilling them, but the same cannot be said of liquids.

   Rewrite, beginning with

   <u>Unlike liquids,</u>

   The next words will be

   A. it is easy to

   B. we can easily

   C. solid objects can easily be

   D. solid objects are easy to be

7. Although the sandpiper is easily frightened by noise and light, it will bravely resist any force that threatens its nest.

   Rewrite, beginning with

   <u>The sandpiper is easily frightened by noise and light,</u>

The next words will be

A. but it will bravely resist

B. nevertheless bravely resisting

C. and it will bravely resist

D. even if bravely resisting

8. If he had enough strength, Todd would move the boulder. Rewrite, beginning with

Todd cannot move the boulder

The next words will be

A. when lacking

B. because he

C. although there

D. without enough

9. The band began to play, and then the real party started.

Rewrite, beginning with

The real party started

The next words will be

A. after the band began

B. and the band began

C. although the band began

D. the band beginning

10. Chris heard no unusual noises when he listened in the park.

Rewrite, beginning with

Listening in the park,

The next words will be

A. no unusual noises could be heard

B. then Chris heard no unusual noises

C. and hearing no unusual noises

D. Chris heard no unusual noises

Reading Comprehension

In an ACCUPLACER placement test, there are 20 questions of two primary types in Reading Comprehension.

- The first type of question consists of a reading passage followed by a question based on the text. Both short and long passages are provided. The reading passages can also be classified according to the kind of information processing required, including explicit statements related to the main idea, explicit statements related to a secondary idea, application, and inference.

- The second type of question, sentence relationships, presents two sentences followed by a question about the relationship between these two sentences. The question may ask, for example, if the statement in the second sentence supports that in the first, if it contradicts it, or if it repeats the same information.

Reading Comprehension Sample Questions

Read the statement or passage and then choose the best answer to the question. Answer the question based on what is stated or implied in the statement or passage.

1. In the words of Thomas De Quincey, "It is notorious that the memory strengthens as you lay burdens upon it." If, like most people, you have trouble recalling the names of those you have just met, try this: The next time you are introduced, plan to remember the names. Say to yourself, "I'll listen carefully; I'll repeat each person's name to be sure I've got it, and I will remember." You'll discover how effective this technique is and probably recall those names for the rest of your life.

    The main idea of the paragraph maintains that the memory

    A. always operates at peak efficiency.

    B. breaks down under great strain.

    C. improves if it is used often.

    D. becomes unreliable if it tires.

2. Unemployment was the overriding fact of life when Franklin D. Roosevelt became president of the United States on March 4, 1933. An anomaly of the time was that the government did not systematically collect statistics of joblessness; actually it did not start doing so until 1940. The Bureau of Labor Statistics later estimated that 12,830,000 persons were out of work in 1933, about one-fourth of a civilian labor force of more than 51 million.

    Roosevelt signed the Federal Emergency Relief Act on May 12, 1933. The president selected Harry L. Hopkins, who headed the New York relief program, to run FERA. A gifted administrator, Hopkins quickly put the program into high gear. He gathered a small staff in Washington and brought the state relief organizations into the FERA system. While the agency tried to provide all the necessities, food came first. City dwellers usually got an allowance for fuel, and rent for one month was provided in case of eviction.

    This passage is primarily about

    A. unemployment in the 1930s.

    B. the effect of unemployment on United States families.

    C. President Franklin D. Roosevelt's presidency.

    D. President Roosevelt's FERA program.

3. It is said that a smile is universally understood. And nothing triggers a smile more universally than a taste of sugar. Nearly everyone loves sugar. Infant studies indicate that humans are born with an innate love of sweets. Based on statistics, a lot of people in Great Britain must be smiling because on average, every man, woman, and child in that country consumes 95 pounds of sugar each year.

    From this passage it seems safe to conclude that the English

A. do not know that too much sugar is unhealthy.

B. eat desserts at every meal.

C. are fonder of sweets than most people.

D. have more cavities than any other people.

4. With varying success, many women around the world today struggle for equal rights. Historically, women have achieved greater equality with men during periods of social adversity. The following factors initiated the greatest number of improvements for women: violent revolution, world war, and the rigors of pioneering in an undeveloped land. In all three cases, the essential element that improved the status of women was a shortage of men, which required women to perform many of society's vital tasks.

We can conclude from the information in this passage that
A. women today are highly successful in winning equal rights.

B. only pioneer women have been considered equal to men.

C. historically, women have only achieved equality through force.

D. historically, the principle of equality alone has not been-enough to secure women equal rights.

5. In 1848, Charles Burton of New York City made the first baby carriage, but people strongly objected to the vehicles because they said the carriage operators hit too many pedestrians. Still convinced that he had a good idea, Burton opened a factory in England. He obtained orders for the baby carriages from Queen Isabella II of Spain, Queen Victoria of England, and the Pasha of Egypt. The United States had to wait another 10 years before it got a carriage factory, and only 75 carriages were sold in the first year.

Even after the success of baby carriages in England,

A. Charles Burton was a poor man.

B. Americans were still reluctant to buy baby carriages.

C. Americans purchased thousands of baby carriages.

D. the United States bought more carriages than any other country.

6. All water molecules form six-sided structures as they freeze and become snow crystals. The shape of the crystal is determined by temperature, vapor, and wind conditions in the upper atmosphere. Snow crystals are always symmetrical because these conditions affect all six sides simultaneously.

The purpose of the passage is to present

A. a personal observation.

B. a solution to a problem.

C. actual information.

D. opposing scientific theories.

Direction for questions 7–10

For the questions that follow, two underlined sentences are followed by a question or statement. Read the sentences, then choose the best answer to the question or the best completion of the statement.

7. The Midwest is experiencing its worst drought in 15 years. Corn and soybean prices are expected to be very high this year.

What does the second sentence do?

A. It restates the idea found in the first.

B. It states an effect.

C. It gives an example.

D. It analyzes the statement made in the first.

8. Social studies classes focus on the complexity of our social environment.

The subject combines the study of history and the social sciences and promotes skills in citizenship.

What does the second sentence do?

A. It expands on the first sentence.

B. It makes a contrast.

C. It proposes a solution.

D. It states an effect.

9. Knowledge of another language fosters greater awareness of cultural diversity among the peoples of the world.

Individuals who have foreign language skills can appreciate more readily other peoples' values and ways of life.

How are the two sentences related?

A. They contradict each other.

B. They present problems and solutions.

C. They establish a contrast.

D. They repeat the same idea.

10. Serving on a jury is an important obligation of citizenship.

Many companies allow their employees paid leaves of absence to serve on juries.

What does the second sentence do?

A. It reinforces what is stated in the first.

B. It explains what is stated in the first.

C. It expands on the first.

D. It draws a conclusion about what is stated in the first.

WritePlacer®

This test measures your ability to write effectively, which is critical to academic success.

Your writing sample will be scored on the basis of how effectively it communicates a whole message to the readers for the stated purpose. Your score will be based on your ability to express, organize, and support your opinions and ideas, not the position you take on the essay topic. The following five characteristics of writing will be considered:

- Focus—The clarity with which you maintain your main idea or point of view
- Organization—The clarity with which you structure your response and present a logical sequence of ideas
- Development and Support—The extent to which you elaborate on your ideas and the extent to which you present supporting details
- Sentence Structure—The effectiveness of your sentence structure
- Mechanical Conventions—The extent to which your writing is free of errors in usage and mechanics

WritePlacer Sample Topic

Prepare a multiple-paragraph writing sample of about 300–600 words on the topic below. You should use the time available to plan, write, review, and edit what you have written. Read the assignment carefully before you begin to write.

Some schools require each student to participate in an organized school sport chosen by the student. People at these schools argue that athletics is an important part of the educational experience and that there should be a rule requiring participation. Others argue that students should be free to decide whether or not they wish to participate in organized school sports. Write an essay for a classroom instructor in which you take a position on whether participation in organized school athletics should be required. Be sure to defend your position with logical arguments and appropriate examples. Your essay must be 300–600 words in length.

Arithmetic

This test measures your ability to perform basic arithmetic operations and to solve problems that involve fundamental arithmetic concepts. There are 17 questions on the Arithmetic tests, divided into three types.

- Operations with whole numbers and fractions: Topics included in this category are addition, subtraction, multiplication, division, recognizing equivalent fractions and mixed numbers, and estimating.

- Operations with decimals and percents: Topics include addition, subtraction, multiplication, and division with decimals. Percent problems, recognition of decimals, fraction and percent equivalencies, and problems involving estimation are also given.

- Applications and problem solving: Topics include rate, percent, and measurement problems; simple geometry problems; and distribution of a quantity into its fractional parts.

Arithmetic Sample Questions

Solve the following problems and select your answer from the choices given. You may use the paper you have been given for scratch paper.

1. $2.75 + .003 + .158 =$
   A. 4.36
   B. 2.911
   C. 0.436
   D. 2.938

2. $7.86 \times 4.6 =$
   A. 36.156
   B. 36.216

   C. 351.56

   D. 361.56

3. $\frac{7}{20} =$

   A. 0.035

   B. 0.858

   C. 0.35

   D. 3.5

4. Which of the following is the least?

   A. 0.105

   B. 0.501

   C. 0.015

   D. 0.15

5. All of the following are ways to write 25 percent of N EXCEPT

   A. 0.25 N

   B. $\frac{25N}{100}$

   C. $\frac{1}{4}$N

   D. 25 N

6. Which of the following is closest to 27.8×9.6?

   A. 280

   B. 300

   C. 2,800

   D. 3,000

7. A soccer team played 160 games and won 65 percent of them. How many games did it win?

   A. 94

   B. 104

   C. 114

   D. 124

8. Three people who work full-time are to work together on a project, but their total time on the project is to be equivalent to that of only one person working full-time. If one of the people is budgeted for one-half of his time to the project and a second person for one-third of her time, what part of the third worker's time should be budgeted to this project?

   A. $\frac{1}{3}$

   B. $\frac{3}{5}$

   C. $\frac{1}{6}$

   D. $\frac{1}{8}$

9. 32 is 40 percent of what number?

   A. 12.8

   B. 128

   C. 80

   D. 800

10. $3\frac{1}{3} - 2\frac{2}{5} =$

   A. $1\frac{1}{2}$

   B. $\frac{1}{15}$

   C. $\frac{14}{15}$

   D. $1\frac{1}{15}$

Elementary Algebra

A total of 12 questions of three types are administered in this test.

- The first type involves operations with integers and rational numbers, and includes computation with integers and negative rationals, the use of absolute values, and ordering.

- The second type involves operations with algebraic expressions using evaluation of simple formulas and expressions, and adding and subtracting monomials and polynomials. Questions involve multiplying and dividing monomials and

polynomials, the evaluation of positive rational roots and exponents, simplifying algebraic fractions, and factoring.
- The third type of question involves translating written phrases into algebraic expressions and solving equations, inequalities, word problems, linear equations and inequalities, quadratic equations (by factoring), and verbal problems presented in an algebraic context.

Elementary Algebra Sample Questions

Solve the following problems and select your answer from the choices given. You may use the paper you have been given for scratch paper.

1. If A represents the number of apples purchased at 15 cents each, and B represents the number of bananas purchased at 10 cents each, which of the following represents the total value of the purchases in cents?

   A. A+B

   B. 25(A+B)

   C. 10A+15B

   D. 15A+10B

2. $\sqrt{2} \times \sqrt{15} = ?$

   A. 17

   B. 30

   C. $\sqrt{30}$

   D. $\sqrt{17}$

3. What is the value of the expression $2x^2 + 3xy - 4y^2$ when $x = 2$ and $y = -4$?

   A. -80

   B. 80

   C. -32

   D. 32

4. In the figure below, both circles have the same center, and the radius of the larger circle is R. If the radius of the smaller circle is 3 units less than R, which of the following represents the area of the shaded region?

    A. πR^2

    B. $\pi(R-3)^2$

    C. $\pi R^2 - \pi \times 3^2$

    D. $\pi R^2 - \pi(R-3)^2$

5. $(3x-2y)^2 =$

    A. $9x^2 - 4y^2$

    B. $9x^2 - 4y^2$

    C. $9x^2 + 4y^2 - 6xy$

    D. $9x^2 + 4y^2 - 12xy$

6. If x > 2, then $\dfrac{x^2 - x - 6}{x^2 - 4} =$

    A. $\dfrac{x-3}{2}$

    B. $\dfrac{x-3}{x-2}$

    C. $\dfrac{x-3}{x+2}$

    D. $\dfrac{3}{2}$

7. $\dfrac{4-(-6)}{-5} =$

    A. $\dfrac{2}{5}$

    B. $-\dfrac{2}{5}$

    C. 2

    D. -2

8. If $2x - 3(x+4) = -5$, then $x =$

    A. 7

    B. -7

C. 17

D. −17

9. $-3(5 - 6) - 4(2 - 3) =$

A. −7

B. 7

C. −1

D. 1

10. Which of the following expressions is equivalent to $20 - \frac{4}{5}x \geq 16$?

A. $x \leq 5$

B. $x \geq 5$

C. $x \geq 32\frac{1}{2}$

D. $x \leq 32\frac{1}{2}$

College-Level Mathematics Test ━━━

The College-Level Mathematics test measures your ability to solve problems that involve college-level mathematics concepts. There are six content areas measured on this test: (a) Algebraic Operations, (b) Solutions of Equations and Inequalities, (c) Coordinate Geometry, (d) Applications and other Algebra Topics, (e) Functions, and (f) Trigonometry. The Algebraic Operations content area includes the simplification of rational algebraic expressions, factoring and expanding polynomials, and manipulating roots and exponents. The Solutions of Equations and Inequalities content area includes the solution of linear and quadratic equations and inequalities, systems of equations, and other algebraic equations. The Coordinate Geometry content area presents questions involving plane geometry, the coordinate plane, straight lines, conics, sets of points in the plane, and graphs of algebraic functions. The Functions content area includes questions involving polynomial, algebraic, exponential, and logarithmic functions.

The Trigonometry content area includes trigonometric functions. The Applications and other Algebra Topics content area contains complex numbers, series and sequences, determinants, permutations and combinations, factorials, and word problems. A total of 20 questions are administered on this test.

Sample Questions

Solve the problem. Use the paper you were given for scratchwork.

1. $2^{\frac{5}{2}} - 2^{\frac{5}{2}}$

    A. $2^{\frac{1}{2}}$

    B. 2

    C. $2^{\frac{3}{2}}$

    D. $2^{\frac{5}{3}}$

    E. 2^2

2. If $a \neq b$ and $\frac{1}{x} + \frac{1}{a} = \frac{1}{b}$ then $x =$

    A. $\frac{1}{b} - \frac{1}{a}$

    B. $b - a$

    C. $\frac{1}{ab}$

    D. $\frac{a-b}{ab}$

    E. $\frac{ab}{a-b}$

3. If $3x^2 - 2x + 7 = 0$, then $\left(x - \frac{1}{3}\right)^2 =$

    A. $\frac{20}{9}$

    B. $\frac{7}{9}$

    C. $-\frac{7}{9}$

    D. $-\frac{8}{9}$

    E. $-\frac{20}{9}$

4. The graph of which of the following equations is a straight line parallel to the graph of $y = 2x$?

    A. $4x - y = 4$

    B. $2x - 2y = 2$

C. $2x - y = 4$

D. $2x + y = 2$

E. $x - 2y = 4$

5. An equation of the line that contains the origin and the point (1, 2) is

   A. $y = 2x$

   B. $2y = x$

   C. $y = x - 1$

   D. $y = 2x + 1$

   E. $\frac{y}{2} = x - 1$

6. An apartment building contains 12 units consisting of one- and two-bedroom apartments that rent for $360 and $450 per month, respectively. When all units are rented, the total monthly rental is $4,950. What is the number of two-bedroom apartments?

   A. 3

   B. 4

   C. 5

   D. 6

   E. 7

7. If the two square regions in the figures below have the respective areas indicated in square yards, how many yards of fencing are needed to enclose the two regions?

A. $4\sqrt{130}$

B. $20\sqrt{10}$

C. $24\sqrt{5}$

D. 100

E. $104\sqrt{5}$

8. If $\log_{10}x = 3$, then $x =$

   A. 3^{10}

   B. 1,000

   C. 30

   D. $\frac{10}{3}$

   E. $\frac{3}{10}$

9. If $f(x) = 2x + 1$ and $g(x) = \frac{x-1}{2}$, then $f(g(x)) =$

   A. x

   B. $\frac{x-1}{4x+2}$

   C. $\frac{4x+2}{x-1}$

   D. $\frac{5x+1}{2}$

   E. $\frac{(2x+1)(x-1)}{2}$

10. If θ is an acute angle and $\sin\theta = \frac{1}{2}$, then $\cos\theta =$

    A. -1

    B. 0

    C. $\frac{1}{2}$

    D. $\frac{\sqrt{3}}{2}$

    E. 2

ACCUPLACER ESL Reading Skills Test

The ESL Reading Skills test measures your ability to read English. Specifically it assesses your comprehension of short passages. It contains brief passages of 50 words or less and moderate length passages of 50 to 90 words. Half of this test contains straightforward comprehension items (paraphrase, locating information, vocabulary on a phrase level, and pronoun reference). The other half assesses inference skills (main idea, fact versus opinion, cause/effect logic, identifying irrelevant information, author's point of view, and applying the authors logic to another situation).

Sample Questions

1. Television has been introduced to almost every country in the world, reaching a large number of viewers on every continent. About 600 million people saw the first person walk on the moon, and a billion people watched the twentieth Olympic Games. Television has in many ways promoted understanding and cooperation among people. It does this by showing educational and cultural programs

   According to the passage, which of the following is true?

   A. Television is watched in nearly every country.

   B. Not everybody who had a television set could watch the 1998 World Cup finals.

   C. Watching television makes people dissatisfied with their own lives.

   D. Television was invented in 1980.

2. Janet's parents bought her a new sports car as a birthday present. It was blue. Janet sold her 7-year-old blue pickup truck to a high school student. The truck could not go very fast, but the student was happy with it.

   According to the passage, which of these statements is true?

   A. Janet bought a pickup truck and a sports car.

   B. The pickup truck was faster than the sports car.

   C. The high school student traded cars with Janet.

   D. The pickup truck was older than the sports car.

3. Some of Edward Weston's black-and-white photographs of American nature scenes are considered superb examples of visual art. Indeed, some of his photographs have commanded top prices at art galleries.

   Which of the following best characterizes Weston's photographs?

   A. They belong to famous collectors.

   B. They have been sold in art galleries for large sums of money.

   C. They introduced many Americans to visual art.

   D. They contrast American cities with natural settings.

4. Speaking to a group of people can be a frightening experience. Some speakers cope by looking above the heads of the audience. Others try to imagine that they are talking to a friend. A few try picturing the audience in some non-threatening way such as in their pajamas.

   The author of the passage assumes that speakers should

   A. feel comfortable when addressing an audience.

   B. scare the audience.

   C. encourage people to talk during the speech.

   D. speak only to familiar people.

5. People have different ways of learning. Some are better at making mental pictures of new ideas. Others are more comfortable with writing lists of things to memorize. Certain people can learn best when listening to music, while others need silence to concentrate.

   Which of the following is the main idea of the passage?

   A. Mental pictures help many to learn.

   B. Some people prefer lists to making mental pictures.

   C. To learn well you need to be comfortable.

   D. Different individuals have different ways of acquiring information.

6. Before giving first aid to an accident victim, you should obtain his or her consent. Asking for consent takes a simple question. Say to the victim, "I know first aid, and I can help you until an ambulance arrives. Is that okay?"

   "Asking for consent" means asking for

   A. permission to help the victim.

   B. thanks from the victim.

   C. help from onlookers.

   D. information about the victim's injuries.

7. Jane and Paul are busy for 15 hours a day, 5 days a week going to college and working in a restaurant. They go to sleep at 11 p.m. every day, but on Sunday they take part in dance lessons.

   According to the passage, Jane and Paul spend most of their time

   A. at home.

   B. going to college and working.

   C. taking part in dance lessons.

   D. sleeping.

8. If you hold a piece of copper wire over the flame of a match, heat will be conducted by the copper wire to your fingers, and you will be forced to drop the wire. You will, however, still be able to hold the match because the match is a poor conductor of heat. Anyone, child or adult, can try this simple experiment.

   Which of the following is implied in the passage above?

   A. Copper is a good conductor of heat.

   B. A match and copper conduct heat equally.

   C. A match is an excellent conductor of heat.

   D. Matches should be kept out of the reach of small children.

9. Many people own different pets. Dogs, cats, birds, and fish are common household pets. Others pets are considered to be exotic animals. These include snakes, lizards, and hedgehogs.

   Snakes are

   A. uncommon pets.

   B. likely to be found in a household with dogs.

   C. found only in zoos.

   D. not allowed in people's homes.

10. Cesar Chavez was an influential leader for farmworkers. He fought for their rights and better working conditions. Chavez led many strikes that angered farm owners. Eventually he succeeded in getting increased wages and improved living situations for farmworkers.

    Chavez changed lives because he

    A. helped the farmers get more workers.

    B. worked for the farmers.

    C. helped work on the farms every day.

    D. changed the conditions for the farmworkers.

ACCUPLACER ESL Sentence Meaning Test

The ESL Sentence Meaning test measures how well you understand the meaning of sentences in English. It assesses the understanding of word meanings in one-or two-sentence contexts. The sentences are drawn from the subject areas of natural science, history/social studies, arts/humanities, psychology/human relations, and practical situations. There are four content areas measured: (a) Particle, Phrasal Verbs, Prepositions of Direction; (b) Adverbs, Adjectives, Connectives Sequence; (c) Basic Nouns and Verbs; and (d) Basic and Important Idioms.

Sample Questions

The sentence below has a blank space. Choose the word or phrase that makes the sentence meaningful and correct.

1. Shikibu Murasaki, who wrote almost a thousand years ago, was one of the world's _____ novelists.
   A. most early
   B. too early
   C. more early
   D. earliest

2. The Chang children _____ their parents by making sandwiches for the whole family.
   A. helped out
   B. helped with
   C. helps for
   D. helps to

3. As demonstrated by his last album, which was released after his death, Ibrahim Ferrer _____ one of the most beautiful voices in Latin music.
   A. had
   B. have
   C. have had
   D. having

4. After we saw the play, we had different opinions _____ Jane's performance.
   A. about
   B. at
   C. for
   D. towards

Each problem contains one or two sentences followed by a question. Choose the correct answer to the question.

5. Elena found a tomato that was much bigger than all the others in the garden.

   How did the tomato compare to the others in the garden?

   A. It was the smallest.

   B. It was not very large.

   C. It was larger than some.

   D. It was the largest.

6. When the popular entertainer canceled her appearance, the Latin American festival was postponed indefinitely.

   When will the festival likely take place?

   A. Tonight

   B. Tomorrow

   C. Next week

   D. Many weeks later

7. Janet is never late to meet her friends, and sometimes arrives early.

   Which best describes Janet?

   A. Lonely

   B. Punctual

   C. Talkative

   D. Tardy

8. Bram Stoker is best known for his classic horror novel *Dracula*, which was published in 1897.

   What did Bram Stoker do?

   A. He was a doctor.

   B. He was a merchant.

   C. He was a writer.

   D. He was an engineer.

9. Exhausted from her transatlantic flight, Judy could not stay up past 9 P.M.

   What did Judy do at 9 P.M.?

   A. Leave work

   B. Come home from the airport

   C. Lose her enthusiasm

   D. Go to bed

10. This semester many students are enrolled in a new course, African Dance, which is being taught by a first-time instructor, Sheila Duncan.

    How long has the university offered the African dance class?

    A. For a short time

    B. For many years

    C. For an entire school year

    D. On and off for a while

ACCUPLACER ESL Language Use Test

The ESL Language Use test measures your proficiency in using correct grammar in English sentences. There are five content areas measured on this test: (a) Nouns, Pronouns, Pronoun Case Structure; (b) Subject–Verb Agreement; (c) Comparatives, Adverbs, Adjectives; (d) Verbs; and (e) Subordination/Coordination.

Sample Questions

The sentence below has a blank space. Choose the word or phrase that makes a grammatically correct sentence.

1. _____ washing her sweater, Mary hung it up to dry.
   A. After
   B. Before

C. By

D. Until

2. Some day men and women _____ to Mars.
   A. will travel
   B. will travels
   C. will traveling
   D. will traveled

3. Water _____ at a temperature of zero degrees Celsius.
   A. having frozen
   B. freezing
   C. freeze
   D. freezes

4. _____ get a new haircut?
   A. Have you
   B. Does you
   C. Are you
   D. Did you

5. Jacques Cousteau will be remembered for his inventions andfor _____ to marine science.
   A. dedication
   B. his dedication
   C. being dedicated
   D. his being dedicated

6. Since my parents always insist that I get a good night's sleep, they were _____ when I stayed out last night past my curfew.
   A. very happy
   B. very relieved
   C. very tired
   D. very angry

Read the two sentences below and choose the best way of combining them.

7. Her puppy ran out into the street chasing a cat. The owner quickly went to retrieve it.
   A. The owner quickly went to retrieve it after a cat was chased into the street by her puppy.
   B. The owner quickly retrieved it after her puppy chased a cat into the street.
   C. When her puppy ran into the street after a cat, the owner quickly went to retrieve the puppy.
   D. Quickly retrieving it, the owner went quickly after her puppy that ran out into the street after a cat.

8. Lisa plays the piano. Her sister Kelly plays the piano, too.
   A. Lisa and her sister Kelly plays the piano.
   B. Both Lisa and her sister Kelly play the piano.
   C. Lisa plays the piano and Kelly plays the piano.
   D. Lisa and Kelly too play the piano.

9. The road was slippery. We put chains on the tires.
   A. Although the road was slippery, we put chains on the tires.
   B. The road became slippery when we put chains on the tires.
   C. We put chains on the tires because the road was slippery.
   D. Putting chains on the tires, the road we were on was slippery.

10. Kazuko took her dog for a walk. They went to the park.
   A. Kazuko, going to the park, took her dog for a walk.
   B. Kazuko took her dog for a walk in the park.
   C. Kazuko took her dog for a walk because they went to the park.
   D. Kazuko and her dog went to the park, where they walked.

Answer Key

SENTENCE SKILLS	
QUESTION NUMBER	**CORRECT ANSWER**
1	D
2	A
3	B
4	C
5	B
6	C
7	A
8	B
9	A
10	D

ARITHMETIC	
QUESTION NUMBER	**CORRECT ANSWER**
1	B
2	A
3	C
4	C
5	D
6	A
7	B
8	C
9	C
10	C

READING COMPREHENSION	
QUESTION NUMBER	**CORRECT ANSWER**
1	C
2	D
3	C
4	D
5	B
6	C
7	B
8	A
9	D
10	A

ELEMENTARY ALGEBRA	
QUESTION NUMBER	**CORRECT ANSWER**
1	D
2	C
3	A
4	D
5	D
6	B
7	D
8	B
9	B
10	A

CLM	
QUESTION NUMBER	**CORRECT ANSWER**
1	C
2	E
3	E
4	C
5	A
6	E
7	C
8	B
9	A
10	D

ESL SENTENCE MEANING	
QUESTION NUMBER	**CORRECT ANSWER**
1	D
2	A
3	A
4	A
5	D
6	D
7	B
8	C
9	D
10	A

ESL READING SKILLS	
QUESTION NUMBER	**CORRECT ANSWER**
1	A
2	D
3	B
4	A
5	D
6	A
7	B
8	A
9	A
10	D

ESL LANGUAGE USE	
QUESTION NUMBER	**CORRECT ANSWER**
1	A
2	A
3	D
4	D
5	B
6	D
7	C
8	B
9	C
10	B

Notes

Chapter 2: Affordable for All

1. Becky Yerak, "Student Loan Debt: The Next Economic Time Bomb?" *Chicago Tribune*, April 12, 2012.

Chapter 4: It's Not Where You Study, It's What You Study

1. This chapter draws on statistics from the Bureau of Labor Statistics and other federal government sources. It also owes a debt to the pioneering research of labor economist Anthony P. Carnevale and his colleagues at the Georgetown University Center on Education and the Workforce, especially the following reports: "Help Wanted: Projections of Jobs and Education Requirements Through 2018" (June 15, 2010), "What's It Worth: The Economic Value of College Majors" (May 24, 2011), "The College Payoff: Education, Occupations, Lifetime Earnings" (August 5, 2011), "STEM: Science, Technology, Engineering, Mathematics" (October 20, 2011), "Career Clusters: Forecasting Demand for High School Through College Jobs 2008–2018" (November 14, 2011), "Certificates: Gateway to Gainful Employment and College Degrees" (June 5, 2012), and "Healthcare" (June 21, 2012). They are all available at http://cew.georgetown.edu/publications/reports.

Chapter 5: The Smart Start to a Bachelor's Degree

1. Michael Winerip, "Opening Up a Path to Four-Year Degrees," *New York Times*, April 15, 2012.
2. Ibid.

Chapter 6: Two-Year Degrees and One-Year Professional Certificates

1. Christopher Beam, "Community College Organizer," *Slate*, July 14, 2009, http://www.slate.com/articles/news_and_politics/politics/2009/07/community_college_organizer.html.
2. Complete College America, *Time Is the Enemy*, September 2011, http://www.completecollege.org/docs/Time_Is_the_Enemy.pdf.
3. Complete College America, *Certificates Count: An Analysis of Sub-Baccalaureate Certificates*, December 2010, http://dl.dropbox.com/u/13281059/Other%20Certificates%20Count%20Release%20Docs/Certificates%20Count%20FINAL%2012-05.pdf.
4. Emily Hanford, "Another Kind of Education," American RadioWorks, http://americanradioworks.publicradio.org/features/tomorrows-college/dropouts/another-higher-ed.html.
5. Complete College America, *Certificates Count*.
6. "It Pays to Be Nimble: New Majors at Community Colleges," *Chronicle of Higher Education*, August 31, 2009; see also Mitchell Technical Institute, "Wind Turbine Technology," accessed May 14, 2012, http://www.mitchelltech.edu/ViewProgram.aspx?id=24&ContentID=9.
7. The Tennessee Technology Centers description comes from several sources: Jamie P. Merisotis and Stan Jones, "Degrees of Speed," *Washington Monthly*, May/June 2010; Complete College America, *A Working Model for Student Success: The Tennessee Technology Centers*, June 2010, http://www.completecollege.org/docs/Tennessee%20Technology%20Centers-%20A%20Preliminary%20Case%20Study(1).pdf; Tennessee Higher Education Commission, "Community College Certificate Programs With 90% or Higher Job Placement Rates"; American RadioWorks, "Some College, No Degree," August 2011, http://americanradioworks.publicradio.org/features/tomorrows-college/dropouts/transcript.html.

8. Anthony P. Carnevale, Nicole Smith, and Jeff Stroh, *Help Wanted: Projections of Jobs and Education Requirements Through 2018* (Washington, DC: Georgetown University Center on Education and the Workforce, June 15, 2010), cew.georgetown.edu/jobs2018/.

9. Daniel de Vise, "Want to Earn More Money? Study STEM," *College Inc.* (blog), *Washington Post*, October 28, 2011, www.washingtonpost.com/blogs/college-inc/post/want-to-earn-more-money-study-stem/2011/10/28/gIQALikjPM_blog.html.

Chapter 8: What You Should Do to Prepare for College-Level Work if You Are Now in High School

1. "Ready or Not: Creating a High School Diploma That Counts," *American Diploma Project*, www.achieve.org/ReadyorNot.

2. "Preparing for College," Harvard College Office of Admissions, 2009, http://www.admissions.college.harvard.edu/apply/preparing/index.html.

Chapter 10: The Placement Tests That Determine Where You Start in College

1. Michael Winerip, "In College, Working Hard to Learn High School Material," *New York Times*, October 23, 2011.

2. Fernanda Santos, "College Readiness Is Lacking, City Reports Show," *New York Times*, October 24, 2011.

Appendix: The Higher Education America Needs

1. Collin Eaton, "Job Training in Aerospace Takes Flight at Community College in Washington," *Chronicle of Higher Education*, November 20, 2011, www.chronicle.com/article/Job-Training-in-Aerospace/129852/; Steve Wilhelm, "To Land Boeing's Next Plane Factory, Washington's

Training System Must Drill Down," *Puget Sound Business Journal*, September 23, 2011, washingtonaerospace.com/docs/Puget_Sound_Business_Journal_092311.pdf.

2. Aerospace Futures Alliance of Washington, "The Washington State Aerospace Training and Research Center Exceeds Expectations!," 2010, www.afa-wa.com/trainingcenter.php.

3. Sue Ambler and Heather Villars, "Partnerships That Work," *The Herald* (Everett, WA), August 20, 2011.

4. UPS, "UPS Worldport Facts," http://pressroom.ups.com/Fact+Sheets/UPS+Worldport+Facts.

5. Dana Fischetti, "World-Class Hub," *U of L Magazine*, Winter 1999, www.louisville.edu/ur/ucomm/mags/winter99/ups.html.

6. Complete College America, "Part 3: State Profiles," *Time Is the Enemy*, September 2011, www.completecollege.org/docs/Time_Is_the_Enemy_Profiles.pdf

7. Business-Higher Education Forum, *Learn and Earn: Modeling the Success of Metropolitan College*, 2011, http://www.bhef.com/publica tions/documents/Learn_and_Earn_Report.pdf.

8. Alexander Wilson, "UPS' Work-Study Package," *Forbes*, August 3, 2011.

9. Ibid.

10. The Aspen Institute, "College Excellence Program: Walla Walla Community College," accessed May 14, 2012, www.aspeninstitute.org/policy-work/aspen-prize/WallaWallaCommunityCollege.

11. Economic Modeling Specialists, Inc., *Economic Analysis of the Walla Walla Wine Cluster: Past, Present, and Future*, June 2007, Sowicellars.com/reports/Walla_Walla_Economic_Analysis.pdf.

12. Apprenticeship 2000, www.apprenticeship2000.com. See also Ronnie L. Bryant, "Apprenticeship 2000 Addresses High-tech Needs with Old-world Model," Charlotte Regional Partnership, August 2011, www.charlotteusa.com/news-media/monday-memo/apprenticeship-2000-addresses-high-tech-needs-with-old-world-model.

13. Michael Hirsh and Fawn Johnson, "Desperately Seeking Skills," *National Journal*, August 3, 2011, www.nationaljournal.com/magazine/workers-without-right-education-skills-floundering-in-weak-economy-20110728.

14. Julie Bird, "A Big Investment in Charlotte Youth," *Charlotte Business Journal*, June 17, 2011, www.bizjournals.com/charlotte/print-edition/2011/06/17/a-big-investment-in-youth.html?page=all.

Acknowledgments

In 2007, when I was approached informally about the vacant presidency of Indiana's Ivy Tech Community College system, I was an experienced consumer of employable talent thanks to my business career, but I was a novice in the delivery of education. I knew that Ivy Tech was a unique institution, thanks to its having become the first and by far the largest statewide, singly accredited community college system in the country in 2005. That same year Governor Mitch Daniels, a far-seeing education visionary and as of January of 2013 the twelfth president of Purdue University, signed a landmark Indiana higher education bill that gave new recognition to Ivy Tech's role in both educational attainment and economic development. Beyond these facts, however, I had no real sense of what Ivy Tech and community colleges throughout the country were doing to meet the educational and economic development needs of their regions.

Prior to becoming Ivy Tech's president on July 1, 2007, I went on a 45-day listening tour of Indiana. Visiting community and business groups in the 14 regions into which Ivy Tech's 30 campuses are organized, I heard again and again about the value and opportunity that the institution was creating. Ivy Tech's 14 regional chancellors were critical participants in their respective regions' economic development, and were recognized as such almost to the point of being folk heroes.

When I finished this listening tour, I was shocked how little awareness of the community colleges' role there was at the statewide level in Indiana and nationally. Within a year, the picture began to change dramatically. The Brookings Institution released a short but watershed report on the community college as a vital economic development tool. The Lumina Foundation, the Bill and Melinda Gates Foundation, the Obama administration, and both Republican and Democratic governors, among others, embraced the report, and community colleges began to receive long-overdue attention. The Lumina Foundation, led by adopted Hoosier Jamie P. Merisotis, has amplified the intensity of the discussion by announcing Goal 2025, a campaign to spur a national effort for the United States to regain first place in postsecondary educational attainment.

The result has made this a fortuitous time to lead growth at Ivy Tech, despite severe budgetary pressures, because people have been ready to work together to find the best way forward. Thanks especially to Indiana Commissioner of Higher Education Teresa Lubbers and Indiana Commission of Higher Education board members Dennis Bland and Michael Smith, who inspired me with their dedication to the needs of at-risk students; and to Ivy Tech's advisors in becoming part of the Lumina Foundation's Achieving the Dream initiative, whose mission is to foster community college students' success, including Anne Shane, Ivy Tech state board chair, and State Representative Greg Porter.

Over the past several years, Ivy Tech's administration, faculty, and staff have taken the Ivy Tech story to new levels of success in service to the state of Indiana, and have contributed significantly to the positive impact of community colleges nationally in a host of areas. I am grateful for the opportunity to work with them.

Writing this book has been part and parcel of the collaborative teamwork throughout Ivy Tech. I have drawn heavily on the expertise in varied areas of Ivy Tech's Paul Amador, Rhonda M. Angsman, Ben Burton, Kimberly Wheeler Butts, Delores Hazzard, Saundra Kay King, Dottie Larson, Charles W. Lepper, Amanda Mills, Sabrina Pennington, Jeff L. Pittman, Sandra L. Ward, and Sheila M. Wiggins-Biggs. John Pyzik, Jeffrey Terp, and especially Jeffery Scott Fanter and Lindsey Garner all played important roles in keeping the book on track.

As president of Ivy Tech and as the author of this book, I have benefited enormously from discussions with a diverse group of thought and action leaders who have worked to support and further community colleges' dual mission of educational attainment and economic development, including Brian Bosworth, founder and president of FutureWorks; Walter G. Bumphus, president of the American Association of Community Colleges (AACC); Stan Jones, former Indiana Commissioner of Higher Education and founder and president of Complete College America; Hilary Pennington, the founding president of Jobs for the Future and later the head of the Gates Foundation's postsecondary education initiative; Rod Risley, executive director of Phi Theta Kappa; Tony Zeiss, president of North Carolina's Central Piedmont Community College; and three fellow heads of statewide community college systems—Glenn DuBois, chancellor of the Virginia Community College System; Joe D. May, president of the Louisiana Community and Technical College System; and R. Scott Ralls, president of the North Carolina Community College System—who have joined me in cofounding a new advocacy coalition of community colleges, Rebuilding America's Middle Class (RAMC), which convened its first annual meeting in Indianapolis on June 4, 2012, and will complement the work of the AACC.

Terrell Halaska, principal at HCM Strategists, and her colleague Iris Palmer have provided invaluable expertise in educational policy making at both the state and national level and given me helpful feedback on the content and scope of this book.

Anthony Carnevale has been especially generous in sharing the data on educational attainment and career and employment opportunities that he and his colleagues at the Georgetown University Center on Education and the Workforce have compiled and mined for important insights into transformative trends in the economy and their impact on higher education.

A special thanks to Joe Tessitore and Mary Frances Duffy of the Dilenschneider Group. Drawing on his experience as a senior publishing executive, Joe nimbly guided me through the strange new world of writing a book, and Mary Frances capably took on a variety of editorial, marketing, and research roles. Thanks also to Hilary Hinzmann for his editorial assistance in putting the book together, and to David Hill and Drew Lindsay for their editorial contributions.

At John Wiley & Sons, Inc., I want to thank Richard Narramore, my deft, insightful editor, for his belief in the book and help in shaping it, and the rest of the Wiley team.

My wife, Bobbette, executive director of the Leadership Academy of Madison County, a youth and adult leadership organization sponsored by Indiana's Anderson University and the Chamber of Commerce for Anderson and Madison County, has been a personal leadership coach to me, and I am grateful for her advice and counsel during the writing of this book and throughout our lives together.

Thanks, too, to Leland Boren, an inspirational business leader who has mentored me for the past twenty years and who is still on the job at age eighty-nine.

Finally, a number of community college students and graduates, not only from Ivy Tech but from schools across the country, have generously shared stories from their experiences for this book. Thanks to Chrystal Boston, Amanda Carrero, Steve Crist, Pat Cumber, Lorelle Espinosa, Javier Figueras, Cathy Hendrickson, Victoria Hirsh, Sarah Hubert, Tricia Jenkins, Tyler Martin, Edward Mass, Heather Naugler, Makisha Noel, Jennifer Papworth, Delores Petroulas, Tina Pittman, Michael Rice, Fernando Schiefelbein, Kwame Walker, Andrew Wangemann, Joseph Washenko, Sherron Washington, Tenaha Williams, and Jessie Wixon. The achievements of these and countless other community college students are this book's true reason for being.

Index

Additional resources for educational websites start at page 175.